I0491490

CONTENTS

WELCOME TO EBAY UNLOCKED

About the Author

I have had a love affair with Small Business since I started my first one while in college. I enjoy building new businesses and I try to surround myself with super-talented people that help make the magic happen. I currently have interests in the following markets: Consulting & Mentoring, Vacation Rentals, Social Commerce and Marketplace Selling, Podcasts, Fishing, and Waterfowl Hunting.

I co-host The Small Business Show podcast each week and I create content, guides and books related to topics I am interested in.

Learn more and connect with me at

https://shannonjean.com

Cheers to your inevitable success!

AN EBAY LIFE

It was an early morning dilemma back in 1999 that led me to eBay. I found myself stuck with several hundred Mac LC power supplies that I had no idea how to sell. I had overextended my cash reserves to buy the power supplies because I just knew that they were a great deal. My business, MacResQ, was brand new, and I was stressed.

I had poked around the eBay website a bit but had not used the service before that stressful day in '99 when I snapped a few photos and uploaded them to the marketplace.

I sold those power supplies – all of them – to one person within the first 24-hours of listing them for sale. After that sale, I realized two important things. First, I had priced the power supplies too low! Second, I needed to learn more about eBay and add it to my talent stack to be successful.

eBay is much more than just a marketplace. It's a community of supportive sellers, a vast treasure trove of worldwide buyers, as well as a people connection engine that can bring you together with powerful, life-changing resources. eBay is a comprehensive research tool that can help you with your business like mine back in 1999. eBay is also a massively dynamic study guide to help you test, iterate and create revenue streams that can give you the freedom to live the charmed life you have always wanted.

Since those first sales, I have made eBay a part of just about every business I have created over the past 25+ years as a Small Business owner. I have spoken at eBay events, been featured in eBay marketing commercials, met with eBay CEOs, and advised thousands of Small Businesses each week on The Small Business Show podcast.

eBay Unlocked shares my story of success that goes far beyond just selling. Join me as I share how to unlock the secrets of connecting with buyers and sellers throughout the world, re-searching what products to sell and where to buy them, how to connect with the supportive community that can propel your success, and much more.

Join the Unlocked Community

This book is a roadmap to help you find success on eBay. What can help you even more is a community of supportive sellers growing their businesses on marketplaces like eBay, Poshmark, and beyond.

There is no charge to join the Unlocked group. The private group is open to anyone that has purchased eBay Unlocked or

Poshmark Unlocked. Join hundreds of other sellers that have found help in our community, ask questions and lift each other up as we all find success.

I hope to see you in the group soon!

Join here:

https://www.facebook.com/groups/poshmarkunlocked

INTRODUCTION

Before you start eBay Unlocked, please take a few minutes to re-view the following:

What you will learn in the pages of eBay Unlocked:

eBay Unlocked is all about helping you create success on eBay. You will find techniques and tips about all the fundamental parts of starting a business or improving an existing business on eBay.

But it's also about much more. Throughout the book, you will learn why eBay is such a powerful partner to help you succeed both on eBay and in the real world. I want you to take away this concept beyond just selling products on the eBay marketplace. By connecting to the eBay community and learning beyond just buying and selling, I hope to convince you about eBay's real power and how it can change your life by building wealth and knowledge and connecting you with other eBay business owners, eBay executives, and more. This path has worked for me, and I know it can work for you.

Beyond the book, I want to connect with you myself. After 25+ years as a Small Business Owner, I thoroughly enjoy meeting new entrepreneurs like yourself and helping them to succeed. I will show you how to connect with me via LinkedIn and use that platform to build relationships with other eBay sellers, eBay employees, and executives to help you succeed. I will also connect with you via the private Unlocked Group, and you can reach me via email anytime at me@shannonjean.com.

A bit of housekeeping before you start eBay Unlocked:

Photos and images: If you are reading the paperback version of eBay Unlocked, some of the pictures may be blurry. Please contact me at the email address below, and I will gladly send you a PDF version of the book with crisp and clear images for your use.

Connect with me here: me@shannonjean.com

Your Mileage May Vary: These tactics and Best Practices have consistently worked well for me during the 18-years I have been selling on eBay. I do not have all the answers. I can only share with you what techniques have worked for me and my businesses. I welcome your feedback, corrections, and suggestions.

This stuff works! I will always share my results, showing my earnings, sales information, and other confidential info with you so you can see that these tactics work and that I practice what I preach. I don't share this info to brag about my success but rather inspire you to find your success, however you define it.

Dip in and out: You may find it useful to read this book from start to finish or jump around to different sections. Whatever works for you!

The Unlocked Business Community: Join hundreds of other sellers helping each other succeed on eBay, Poshmark, and other marketplaces. Get your questions answered and find ongoing support from me and other talented humans at various stages of their path to success.

https://www.facebook.com/groups/poshmarkunlocked/

Poshmark Unlocked: As part of your success system, I highly recommend selling on multiple marketplaces. My first book, Poshmark Unlocked, has helped thousands of sellers find success on the Poshmark marketplace. You can learn more at https://shannonjean.com/books

Copyright © 2021 Shannon Jean

All rights reserved. No part of this publication may be reproduced, distributed, or transmitted in any form by any means including photocopying, recording or other electronic or mechanical methods, without the prior written permission of the publisher and copyright holder, except in the case of brief quotations embodied in reviews and certain other non-commercial uses permitted by copyright law.

Ready to learn how to create your system to succeed on eBay? Let's go!

CREATING YOUR EBAY ACCOUNT.

NOW is the time to open your eBay account. Not tomorrow, not next week, not when you learn more. Now. Read this short chapter and then stop reading, set the book down, and create your account.

Why now?

Success is all about ACTION. You can read all about being successful, think about all your great ideas, and dream about attaining your goals, but it's all just a fantasy without action. The first step towards success on eBay is taking action to create your account.

If you already have an eBay account, congrats! You may still want to browse this chapter for some tips about account setup that may be helpful.

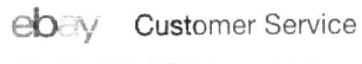

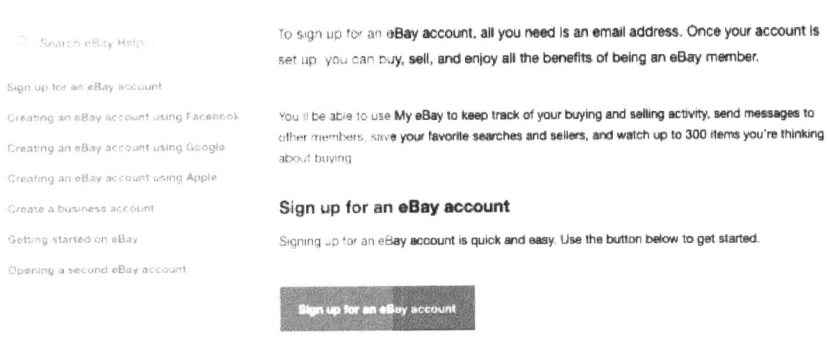

Set up a new account here:
https://www.ebay.com/help/account#account-getting-started

Don't wait until you finish this book to set up your new eBay account! Get your eBay account setup now to begin building credibility and history with eBay. When you first create your eBay account, you will have limits on how much you can sell (more on selling limits later).

eBay doesn't know you. eBay does not know how awesome you are, how honest you are, and how good your intentions are. Getting your account open starts the clock ticking – the older your account is, the more credibility you will have with eBay.

Choosing an eBay user name.

You want to select a name that is related to your business. Even if your business is brand new and without a name, an eBay user name should help create trust and credibility with your potential buyers.

Which account name would you be more comfortable buying

from?

Rijckmn-2

or

Fall-River-Saddles

Choose a name that closely references your business or industry. Remember that tens of thousands of potential buyers will be looking at all aspects of your eBay account and sale listings to learn more about you, your business, and your credibility.

Business or Personal?

You are here to build a successful business on eBay. Even if you are starting small, you want to start as a business. During account creation, you will be able to select from a personal or business account.

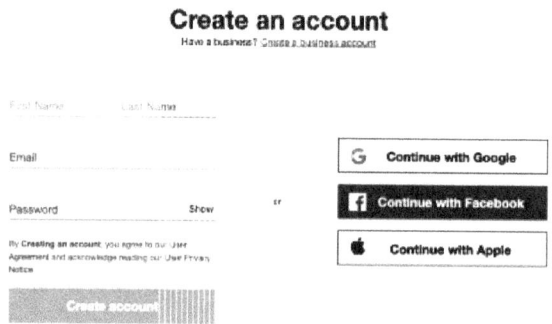

https://signup.ebay.com/pa/crte

When you create your new account, eBay will automatically set you up as an individual seller. After jumping through a few verification hoops (email and phone number), you can go to your eBay settings and change the account type of Business

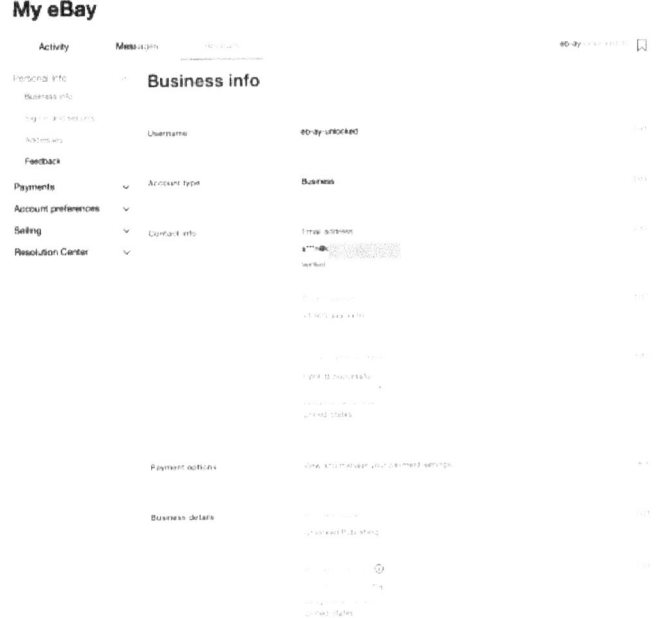

Create your eBay About Me page.

The About Me page is one more chance to tell your story to pro-spective buyers. What message do you want them to see while they are doing research about you? Do you have a compelling story for starting your business (you should)? Do you donate part of your profits to a charity? Are you starting your company to pay for your kid's college tuition? Do you have a long trad-ition of building XX that you are now going to offer on eBay?

Think about the narrative you want to create on eBay. Use the About Me page as an opportunity to be authentic and to build trust with your prospective buyers.

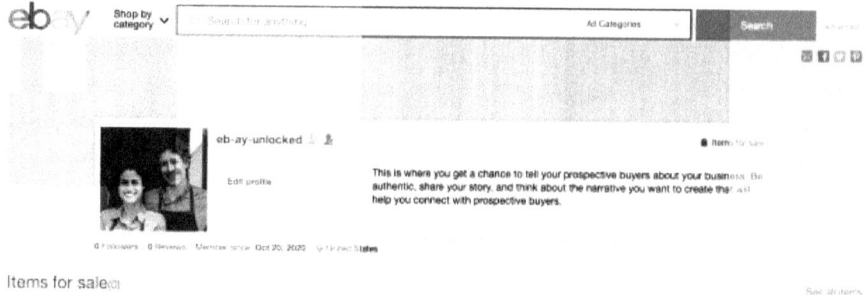

https://www.ebay.com/usr/eb-ay-unlocked

You have a small text area to share some info about your business and yourself. Here's a couple of examples. Think about which one connects with you more:

"We are a huge successful company with the best products, and our goal is to offer the lowest prices and the best service possible."

Or:

"Ted and Mary Watson have been creating hand-made leather products for over a decade. We specialize in western leather styles and are offering many of our more popular designs on eBay. We use the proceeds of these sales towards our children's college fund."

You will read these words over and over in this book: **Tell your story whenever you can.** On your About Me page, on each of your product listings, on the note, you put inside each of your shipments. Your story makes you unique, builds credibility, and connects you with your customers.

Your Account Photo

Which type of photo builds more trust with you?

This   Not This

You are trying to stand out on eBay from other sellers; taking the extra time to build your account details out like this will pay off tremendously. Use a photo that reflects who you are is a great way to create trust with prospective buyers.

Once you have your About Me page setup, eBay will then high-light all of your listings on this page.

Back to Account Setup, there are various options and info to enter https://accountsettings.ebay.com/profile

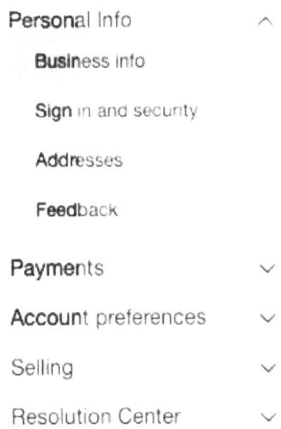

Business Info

Sign in and Security: set up some security questions to protect your account (highly recommended) along with other various security options. I also suggest turning on Two-Factor authentication to protect your account.

Addresses: keep your registration address and your shipping address updated. Any returns will come back to your ship from address.

Feedback: A quick link to items you have sold that are waiting for you to leave feedback about the buyer—more on Feedback in a later chapter.

Payment options: how will you pay for your eBay selling fees? Most fees will come from your pending sales balance (more on that in the payments chapter), but it's a good idea to have a backup payment listed, such as a credit card.

Payments

You can link a Paypal account to allow your customers to pay via Paypal (see the Payments section for more info). You can also set up a Donation account if you would like to donate a percentage of your sales to a cause.

Account Preferences

Site preferences: there are various site preferences you can set up, such as showing product reviews you leave or product guides (You guessed it, more on Reviews and Guides later), bidding rules if you are buying items on this account. It's OK to purchase items from your main eBay account, but just keep in mind that anyone will be able to see your purchase history for the past 90-days. I typically use a different eBay account for buying due to this.

Advertisement preferences: here, you can opt-out of various spammy advertising options.

Communication preferences: This is an important section where you can set up various options about how you want to receive alerts from eBay. I suggest you go through each of the options below:

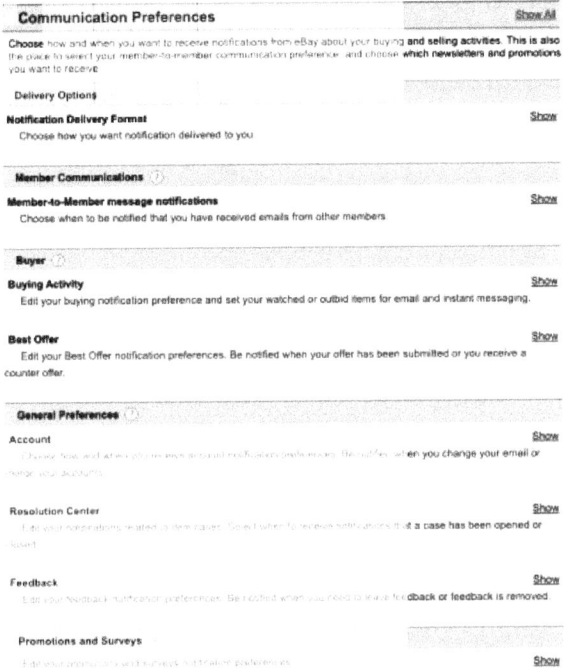

Delivery Options: check your email addresses and update as needed.

Member Communications: select how and when you want to be alerted to inquiries by other eBay members. I suggest you choose Real-time for each of these options.

Buying Activity: select how and when you want to be alerted to issues related to your sales. I suggest you choose Real-time for each of these options.

Best Offer: select how and when you want to be alerted to issues related to offers on your items. I suggest you choose Real-time for each of these options.

General Preferences: various messaging options from eBay. I leave these all at Real-time alerts.

Resolution Center: as part of your epic customer service, you want to leave these settings at Real-time alerts so you can react quickly to any problems.

Feedback: alerts related to feedback on your sales.

Promotions and Surveys: options about how eBay contacts you for various marketing programs.

Payment Options

If you will be purchasing items on eBay from this account, this is where you can enter your payment information.

Selling

Once you make your first sale, you will get access to the Seller Dashboard. We will review how to get that first sale quickly and the Seller Dashboard in a future chapter.

Resolution Center

The Resolution Center is where you will manage any customer service complaints from buyers that you are not able to resolve on your own. I will teach you several methods to avoid this area by turning upset customers into loyal followers. However, sometimes you just can't avoid having a buyer escalate a case to eBay. The Resolution Center is where you can respond and track the progress of open and closed customer service cases.

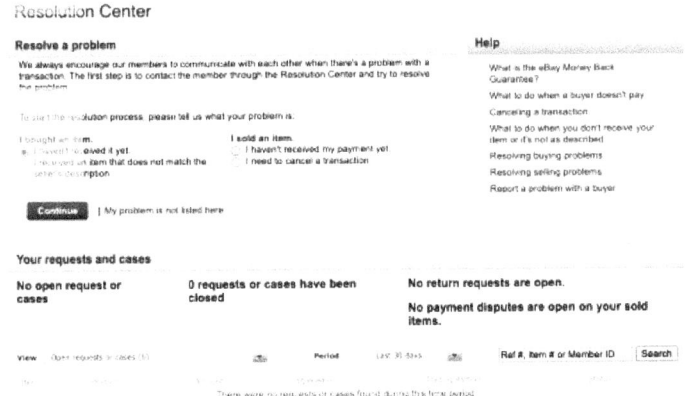

Time to Sell!

You should now have your eBay account created, your email confirmed, and some basic account settings defined. Next, I will walk you through creating your first listing. Let's go!

YOUR FIRST EBAY
PRODUCT LISTING

Before we jump into specific tips about making everything you do on eBay incredible, I want you to create a simple product listing. It doesn't matter what the item is; list something you have sitting on your desk or around your house. The key is taking some action to become familiar with the marketplaces as I walk you through your first listing.

A quick note that eBay is continually updating their platform, and by the time you read this, there may be a new listing experience in place. You can check the rollout of this new listing experience here:
https://community.ebay.com/t5/Announcements/Try-out-the-unified-listing-experience/ba-p/31536605

No one is paying any attention to your new account right now. It's the perfect time to experiment and learn. You will also need to sell at least one item (I will share a shortcut with you on making that first sale in a later chapter) to qualify for Seller Hub. This powerful and centralized seller management tool is free to all eBay sellers that have completed at least one sale.

OK, let's get that first listing up! Grab a product you can sell for $1.00. Pick an item that weighs less than 16 ounces. For this example, grab a pen from your desk to sell.

Click the Sell link at the top of any page on the eBay website.

You can enter data about your item on this page, and eBay will help you find the correct category to sell in. I am going to sell a Montblanc pen for our example.

You can see how eBay is offering up various categories for you to choose. Select the category that closest matches what you are selling. For this example, don't worry about being super accurate with the category. The key is to enter some info, then select a category.

eBay will then offer up some similar products to choose from if your item matches their data. If the matches don't make sense, just click the "Continue without selecting a product" option. In this example, I entered the name of the pen, Montblanc Starwalker, and this is the result eBay brought up.

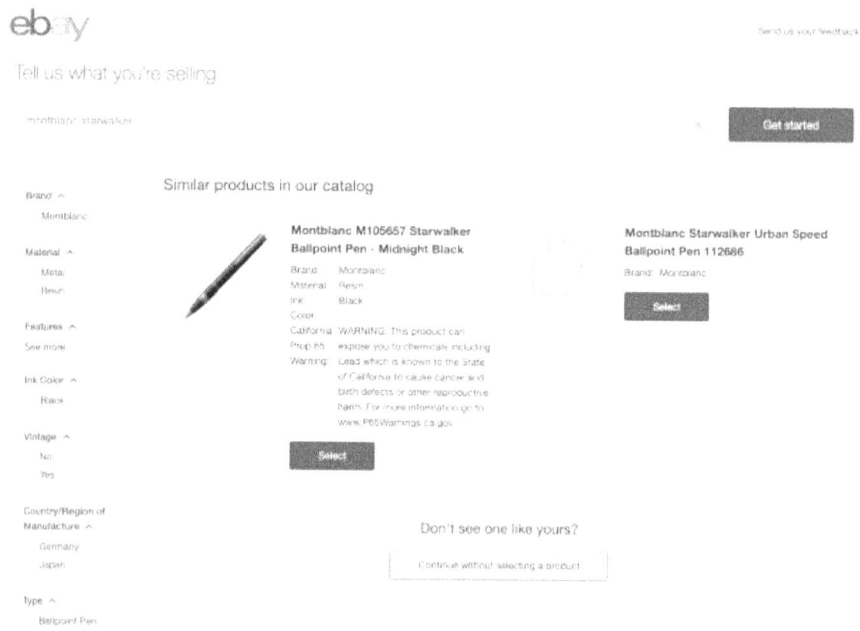

The next screen will be where you will create your listing. It can be a bit overwhelming at first, since there are so many crazy options to choose from – but don't worry! We will go over every-single-option together. We are taking a deep dive into creating your first listing now, but in the future, I will show you how to streamline the listing process by using Templates and Automation that will be super-fast and easy for you to replicate over and over. What will take 10-15 minutes now will take less than a minute once you learn more. OK, let's dive in!

Look for the letters in RED to connect back to the description of the sections below the image.

A – The Listing Title

This is your listing title – you have 80 characters (including spaces) to describe your product in a headline style. You want to use this space wisely! List as many product details as you can since this will help your listings show up in the search results when a potential buyer searches for a term in the listing title.

For example, if you are selling handbags:

Bad: Black Crossbody Purchase

Better: Black Leather Crossbody Purse

Best: New Authentic Tory Burch Alexa Black Leather Crossbody Handbag 36911

The Best example above lists condition, authenticity, brand, color, material, style, and model number— all within the 80-character maximum. **Keep in mind that you are creating listings for eBay users AND search engines.** You want your eBay listings to rank highly on Google when someone searches for any of the terms in your title.

We will be talking more about Keywords and Search Engine Optimization throughout the Guide. The critical thing to keep in mind as you begin to list items for sale is to create content not only for eBay shoppers but also for potential customers searching Google and other search engines for your items. Also, eBay keeps listing information on their marketplace pretty much forever. Even when an item sells or you end a listing, the data is still "live" and can be found with a search on eBay or search engine. This means that your excellent title with all that useful data can continue to drive customers to your business, even after the listing sells.

There are options to add BOLD to your Title for an additional charge – I do not recommend this. Your titles will stand on their own, and adding bold text for $2.00 is not a good investment.

B – Automatic Item Specifics

eBay is crazy for Item Specifics! And rightly so. The Item Specifics that you select for the products you are selling are critically crucial for potential buyers to find your products. There are millions of product listings on eBay and billions of product listings on the Internet. eBay wants to help buyers find your products! The most powerful way that eBay can help you is to standardize specifications about the products you are selling and allow buyers to search for those specifics.

There are many Item Specifics that are required when you list a product for sale. eBay will tell you what those basic specifications are. I highly encourage you to use as many Item Specifics as you can since it will help you in search results.

You are going to read these words over and over in eBay Unlocked: **making your listings easy to find via search on eBay and search engines like Google and one of the most important things you can focus on to make it easier for potential buyers to find your products.**

In section B in the image above, eBay is making some suggestions about possible Item Specifics for the Montblanc pen I am listing for sale in this example. eBay is smart, so I am going to accept all those suggestions.

C – Subtitle

I have mixed feelings about the Subtitle option. It can help your listings stand out and allow you more room to put "headline" type of information that shows up below your product title when people are scrolling through search results. I have had some good results using the subtitle, but not enough where I think the extra fees are justifiable. I suggest you experiment and see how it works for you.

Sidebar – eBay is an incredible place to experiment and try new things. If a product isn't selling for you, make a change! Change the title, add or remove the subtitle, change the angle of your primary photo or change all your photos. You get the idea. If things are working the way you want them with your eBay business, change change change! You can learn a tremendous amount by trying new things and then measuring the results. Be sure to track what happens and measure the results, or else you won't know what works and what doesn't.

D – Category

When you create the product listing, eBay will attempt to assign a category that matches the product. You can change this, but since eBay is pretty smart, they will choose the correct category for you more often than not.

E – Second Category

You will be an additional insertion fee if you add additional categories to list your product in. Since most eBay sales start with a search query, I don't believe you need to worry about listing your products in multiple categories. Your business is unique, and you might experiment with this feature as you grow your business.

F – Variations

Product variations are super powerful and essential if you sell similar items with different variations—clothing, for example. If you have T-shirts with different sizes and colors, you will use Variations to list those options. Otherwise, you would have to create a separate listing for each size and color, which would be crazy and time-consuming.

To use Variations, you have to be selling items as a Fixed Price listing. More about this shortly.

G – Condition

Each category you list products in will have specific product condition types. For this Montblanc example, there are just two options: New and Used. You will find New with tags, New without tags, New with defects, and pre-owned for handbags and other clothing-related products.

Select the right condition for the product you are listing.

Sidebar – About those product conditions. You want to build trust and credibility on eBay. Building trust and credibility take time and a lot of effort. You also want to thrill and pleasantly surprise your customers. Customers are naturally suspicious when buying from new sellers, and they often expect to run into problems with things like shipping time and product condition. If you are selling brand new items, the condition won't be an issue.

If you are selling products with various conditions, be conservative about which condition you choose. If an item has some damage (scratches, scuffs, missing accessories, etc.), you want to point this out clearly and upfront on your product listing. It's all about managing expectations – you want your buyers to be pleasantly surprised rather than bitterly disappointed—more on this in later sections.

H – Photos

As of this writing, you can have up to 12 photos on your product listing. You will add those photos in this section when creating listings directly on the eBay website.

Be sure to read the chapters on photography and photo presentation that are coming up soon. You want to use clear and bright photos without any text, artwork, or borders. Much more about photography is coming up!

You will see the Gallery Plus option below the photos section. This is another upsell on eBay's part that I do not recommend. You will be charged $1.00 for a larger photo that will popup when potential buyers hover their mouse over your main listing photo. Again, I recommend you experiment with Gallery Plus to see if it helps with your particular products.

Sidebar – Copyrighted photos. The quickest way to get product listings flagged and removed is to use photos that you did not take yourself. The only way you can legally use copyrighted images from brands (Gucci, Lulumon, Montblanc, etc.) is to have their written permission. If you have this permission, that's awesome, and you can skip this sidebar! If you don't have permission, brands that may not like having their products listed

on eBay can use this to get your listings removed.
Keep safe and legal. Use your own product photos.

This also goes for text and other graphics. You can't just copy and paste a brand's product detail into your listing. I wish you could, and you may not get hassled when you first start, but you eventually will, and you will thank me for not having to re-do hundreds or thousands of product listings that were removed from eBay.

Learn more about the eBay VeRO program here: https://pages.ebay.com/seller-center/listing-and-marketing/verified-rights-owner-program.html

I – Item Specifics section (see next page for image)

You will see the automatic item specifics that eBay thinks you should add to your product listing. You can leave them as is, remove them all or click the X marks to remove specific specifics. Leave as many as you can. The eBay algorithm loves Item Specifics, and the more you have, the more it will surface your listings in search results.

Item specifics

I

Automatically updated Item specifics   Remove all

Brand: **Montblanc** X   Ink Color: **Black** X
Material: **Leather** X

J   **Required**

Buyers need these item specifics about

*Brand

Montblanc

*Material

Leather

*Ink Color

Black

K   **Additional**

Buyers may also be interested in these

Vintage   187 sea

Features
    Chrome Trim   Gold Trim

    Add

Modified Item ⓘ

    Personalized

Country/Region of Manufacture

California Prop 65 Warning

Type

J – Required Item Specifics

These Item Specifics are required when creating your product listing. The number of required specifics varies by product and category. In this Montblanc example, we must list the Brand, Material that the item is made from, and the Ink Color.

K – Additional Item Specifics

There will be all kinds of additional specifics shown that you can choose for your product listing. Take some time to get to know each one and see if you can enter a value. More is better. List any features, model numbers, colors, where the product was made, etc.

L – Item Description

In this section, you will provide a glorious well-written description of your product. Just kidding – remember PEOPLE DON'T READ. For real. Make it short and to the point. Don't hide any top-secret terms and conditions here because no one will read them.

The Description field is the place to list additional info about the product you are selling. Here's an example of what I put in the description field for a handbag I have for sale right now on eBay:

Here's the link for the listing. Hopefully, it will show as sold by the time you read this! https://www.ebay.com/itm/264860994841

My description (Numbers are there just for reference. See below)

1. New Tory Burch McGraw Slouchy Black Leather Tote

2. Model 41780

3. Store Price $498

4. Authentic Tory Burch model 41780. New without tag. Includes non-branded Dust Bag.

5. A slouchy tote crafted in black pebbled leather with gold-tone hardware. Features 1 interior center zip pocket, 1 slit pocket, 1 zip pocket, an adjustable leather-and-chain shoulder strap with 9.96" drop, a magnetic snap closure. 10.36"H x 13.35"W x 5.98"D. RB8186

6. Enjoy fast shipping and epic customer service from a trusted seller with over 3000 handbags sold to date!

Here's a breakdown of the description:

1: This is a copy of the listing Title. I always include this so potential buyers get a confirmation of what they are buying.

2: I list the product model number to help with additional search results on top of the Item Specifics we discussed above.

3: In this case, I like to show the Store Price. I use the term Store

Price since everyone thinks the Retail Price is never what things sell for.

4: I use this sentence to repeat that the product I am selling is Authentic. I mention the model number again. I then describe the condition once more, along with what accessories or paperwork are included.

5: Here's the actual description that includes some additional specifications, sizing information, and my SKU number that I use to track back to my sales database. I will show you how to add this SKU in another important field in a later section.

6: This is my Credibility Statement. I remind buyers that I ship fast and that I proved epic customer service. I also point out that I am a trusted seller and have been selling on eBay for a long time.

You may find that bullet points and even shorter description details work better for you. Experiment and measure the results!

M – Selling Format

There are two Selling Formats on eBay, Auction, and Fixed-Price. Auctions start at a certain amount from 1 cent on up, and your potential buyers will submit bids for what they want to pay for your product. Fixed Price listings are products you list at specific sale prices for buyers to pay. Let's dig a little deeper.

The format you choose to sell with depends on many factors. A few of which should be:

What brings in the highest return. Do your research on eBay SOLD listings (more on this later) to see what formats bring in the highest sale price. If you have a unique item or a crazy popular product, an auction may generate more excitement and bring in a higher sale price. If your research shows that the products you are selling are bringing in a price you are happy with selling for a fixed price, try that format.

What your cost basis is. If you have a very low cost for an item(s) you are selling, you may want to let them go for whatever the market will pay. eBay auctions are a great way to do this.

Your business model. I know many sellers that put up high volumes of eBay auctions that start at just a penny, and they let them sell for whatever the market is willing to pay. These high-volume sellers play the odds and count on making a large return on investment for some items while not much on others. Is this a good idea for your business? Experiment and measure the results!

I have sold millions of dollars worth of products and services on eBay using both Auction and Fixed-Price selling formats. It's worth experimenting to see which method is right for you.

N – Duration

Select how long you want to list an item for sale:

Auction format: 3, 5, 7 or 10 days.

Fixed Price format: Good 'Til Cancelled. Your product will be listed for sale until you cancel it. Listings renew every month, and you will be charged fees each time the listing relists. See the chapter on Fees for more info.

O – Price

Set your price! For Auctions, list your starting price (the lower the starting price, the more potential buyers you will typically entice. You can also set a Buy It Now price for auction listings. The BIN price is a fixed price that someone can buy the product for. The BIN price is only shown until a buyer places a bid – then it's all auction, all the time. You can also set a Reserve price for your product though I don't recommend it. This hidden (from buyers) dollar amount is the lowest price you will sell an auction listing. Reserve prices typically turn off buyers, and I don't believe it is an effective strategy. eBay also charges additional fees to use the Reserve feature.

For Fixed-Price listings, you will just set your sale price. You can also select to let buyers send you Best Offers. Best offers can help sell your product faster, especially if you have some room to sell for a lower price. Again, experiment, measure, and then decide.

P – Quantity

Enter the quantity you have available to sell. You can also select to sell a quantity as an entire lot for one price.

Q – Private Listing

Select this option if you want bidders and buyers hidden from public view. I don't know why you would do this, but I'm sure there's a great reason. I do not recommend this feature.

R – Make a Donation

You can elect to donate a percentage of your sale to a charity of your choice. Donations can help your sales, and you will get a credit for basic listing fees if you choose this option. eBay will also highlight that you are donating part of your sale to a charity.

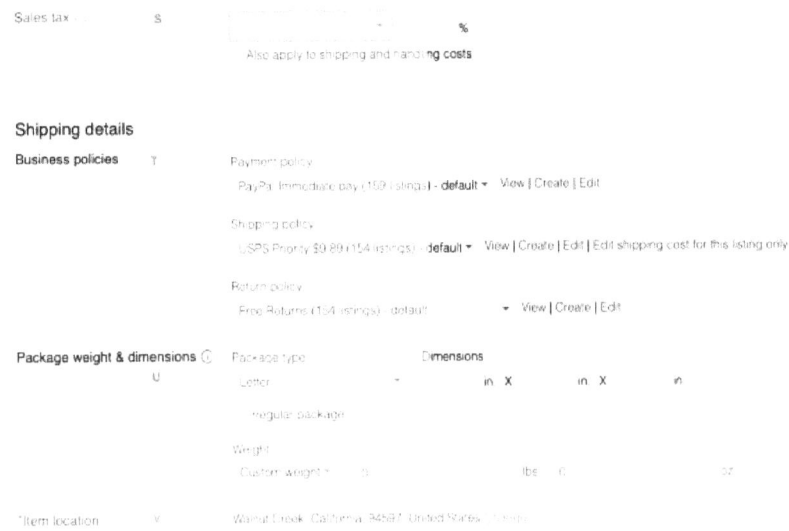

S – Sales Tax

You can leave the Sales Tax selection blank. In 2019 laws were changed, and marketplaces are now required to collect sales tax from sales and remit them to the proper tax authorities on your behalf.

T – Business Policies: Payment, Shipping and Returns

Payment: If you are a new eBay seller, you are automatically enrolled in the latest eBay Managed Payments system. eBay will handle all payment collection on your behalf. Managed Payments overrules any settings in the Payment option. To set up how you would like your funds distributed: https://www.ebay.com/sh/fin/settings

Shipping Policy: You can elect to use a flat-rate shipping charge, offer free shipping, or Calculated Shipping. You can create specific shipping rules for particular items or categories of things you are selling.

You might be thinking, "why would I not just always use Calculated Shipping?" Great question! In my case, I charge a flat rate to keep the shipping price below $10 to encourage sales. Most of the time, the actual shipping charges are $10 or less, sometimes they are more, and I cover the cost difference. Charging for shipping allows me to recoup all or most of the shipping charges if a customer returns an item.

U – Package weight and dimensions

If you are using Calculated Shipping, enter the dimensions and weight of the product you are selling here.

V – Item location:

Item location defaults to your eBay address and is used with Calculated Shipping to come up with the correct shipping rate to charge your customer, based on the product location and their address. If you ship your products from someplace else than your eBay address, change it here to show the correct shipping charges when using Calculated Shipping.

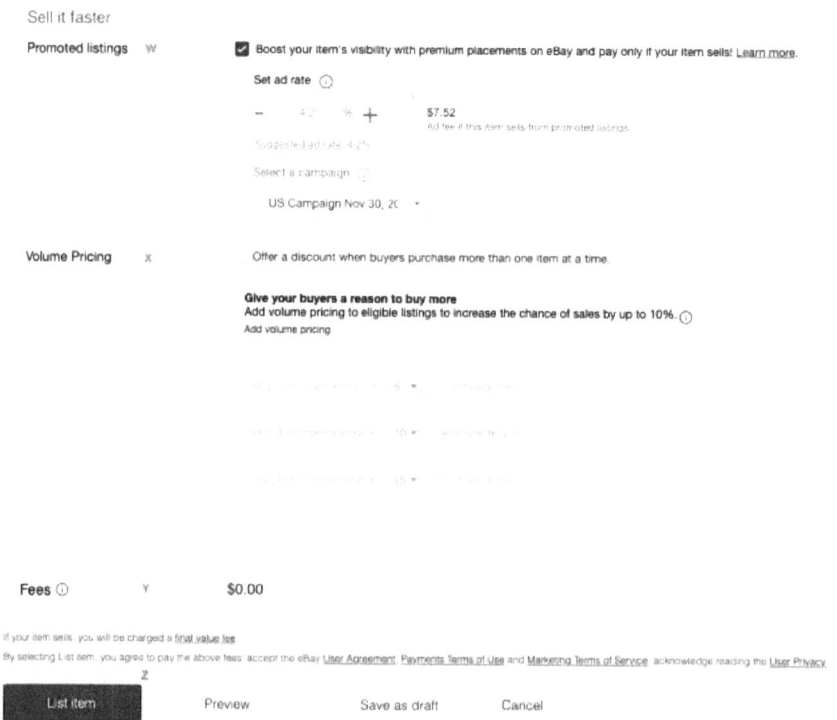

W – Promoted Listings

If you wish to use Promoted Listings to get more exposure for your products, check the box and enter an "ad rate" you want to pay if a product sells that you are promoting.

The ad rate is the percentage IN ADDITION to the regular eBay fees you will pay if a buyer clicks on a Promoted Listing and purchases your item. Be sure to read the chapter on Promoted Listings to get my thoughts on this vital selling option.

If this is your first listing, click the Select a Campaign option to create an ad campaign to track your Promoted Listings. You can create multiple campaigns (perhaps for various product categories you are selling in) or use one campaign for your account.

X – Volume Pricing

Have more than one of a particular product to sell? If the product condition is the same, you can offer discounts when buyers purchase in bulk.

Y – Fees

Click on the $ sign to see a breakdown of listing fees for this listing. Remember that you will also pay selling fees if this product sells. See the chapter on eBay Fees for more information.

Z – List, Preview, or Draft

Click to list this item for sale immediately, or click the Preview button to see what your listing looks like before it goes live. You can also save the work you have done as a draft to come back and finish later.

Before we move on to the next chapter, a quick reminder about SEO and Keywords, this concept is critical and worth revisiting.

When you are creating your listing titles and descriptions, there are some key things to remember:

Product Titles: 85 character maximum. Should contain as much information as possible: Product name, color, model, style – anything unique about the product

Product Description: Complete information – product details, material, color, size info, fit - anything that your customers will find helpful.

Item Specifics: Pull out as many Item Specifics from your description as you can and enter the information into the correct Item Specifics sections.

Use Google Trends (search Google for those words, of course) – search for your product to see what search keywords your potential customers are looking for. These search engine keywords should be part of your title and description.

A word about Search: Over 70% of sales on eBay start with a search. Search for a brand, style, designer, color, category. Keep this in mind when you are creating your SEO and keyword-friendly listing titles and descriptions.

That's it! Remember that this is a manual walkthrough of eBay's built-in listing tool to create a product listing. There are many ways to do this faster and many software tools to increase your productivity instead of using this manual method. I recommend you use this method if you are just getting started – but know that there are lots of other options available that we will discuss later in the book.

SELLING LIMITS FOR NEW EBAY ACCOUNTS

I know you are excited, and you want to immediately list all your inventory on eBay and sell thousands of dollars in the first week. I admire your enthusiasm, and you are on the right track! Unfortunately, there are some speed bumps that eBay has put in your way in the form of selling limits.

Top Takeaway

We'll review your account every month and adjust your limit automatically based on your sales volume and the feedback you receive.

Selling limits are put in place on just about every eBay account. These limits are there to ensure that eBay knows you can handle a particular business volume while taking great care of your customers. Let's discuss this in more detail.

Brand new accounts typically have low selling limits depending on the categories you want to sell in. High-risk categories like fashion or electronics may have lower limits to start than others. You could see a selling limit of $1000-3000 per month to start.

Selling limits are one more reason you want to open your eBay account and start selling something TODAY. Even small sales that you don't make any money on can help you start building your credibility with eBay, so they will be more likely to increase your selling limits.

Don't be frustrated when you find out you can't sell $50K your first month. Remember, eBay doesn't know who you are, and they don't know how good your customer service is. As you make more sales and get more positive feedback, both the dollar amount and the number of items you can sell will increase.

How do you increase your selling limits? You can wait and let eBay review your sales and feedback every 30-days, but I was never patient enough for that. Use the link below to request an increase on your selling limits anytime. Remember that you will have to be continually showing progress to get increased limits: selling more, shipping on time, and getting more positive feedback. It's all related.

Request an increase in your Selling Limit:
https://www.ebay.com/help/selling/listings/selling-limits?id=4107

If you have an existing eBay account with some sales and feedback history, you can also link that account to your new account. Linking accounts is a way for eBay to learn more about you and to increase those limits. Use the link above to submit information about your more established eBay account.

The good news is that you can get Selling Limits decreased quickly by creating great listings and providing great support. Once you have credibility with eBay, they will remove those limits and help you grow. It's always lovely to login into your eBay account and see that you could sell billions of dollars worth of products since eBay trusts you so much.

Monthly limits

10B more items

778 listed and sold / 10B limit on quantity of items

$500B more

$113,240.24 listed and sold / $500B limit

Learn more   Request to list more

FIXED PRICE VS. AUCTION SELLING FORMAT

Most of eBay Unlocked is based on using the Fixed Price selling format to sell your products on eBay. I have sold products in both formats and have found Fixed Price to be more successful for me. That doesn't mean that you shouldn't try auctions for your business. Although over 88% of the products sold on eBay are now Fixed Price, auctions could be a solution for some or all of your business.

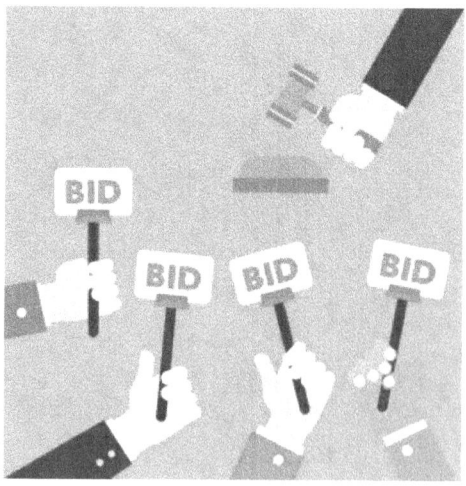

One example of a very successful eBay Auction seller is SaleArea. You can check out their massive volume via this link: https://www.ebay.com/str/salearea

I would also encourage you to use the Sold Items filter to see how many items per day SaleArea moves through auctions. If you have an inexpensive source of product that you need to move large volumes quickly, trying out the auction format may be a great experiment for you.

For Auction Selling Format, a bit of advice:

Don't use Reserve Pricing

Reserve Pricing is when you put a minimum sale price on a product in Auction Format. The reserve is not shown to buyers, and unless the reserve price is exceeded, the product will not sell. Most people don't want to bid on an auction with a Reserve Price since they don't know the hidden minimum sale price for the item.

Use a Minimum Bid

If you have a minimum price you need to get for your product and try Auction Format, you can set a starting bid amount. Being transparent with a starting bid is much more effective than a hidden Reserve Price.

$0.01 Starting Prices

These auctions tend to attract the most attention since buyers think they will get the product for a very low price. However, since there are millions of buyers on eBay, auctions do tend to close at the "market value" of a product. Using $0.01 starting prices can attract many bidders that eventually bid the sale price up to a point where you will make a profitable sale. Experiment, record the results, and adjust as needed.

Do your research

See the chapter on eBay Research before you decide to try Auction Format selling. If you consistently find similar products selling for acceptable prices for your business model, then experimenting with Auction Format may be a good idea. If you find auctions ending with very low sale prices, think twice before listing an item for sale via Auction Format.

Don't offer free shipping with Auction Format

As you will repeatedly read in this book, I am not a fan of the free shipping myth. Buyers will pay reasonable shipping charges for your products. If you are using the $0.01 starting price method, you don't want to get stuck with paying shipping charges if your product sells for less than you anticipated.

Auction Format is just one more thing you can experiment with and decide if it is right for you. Are you currently running a successful business using Auction Format? Reach out to me at me@shannonjean.com and share your story!

BEST OFFER AND THE ART OF NEGOTIATION

Should you use the Best Offer feature when listing your products for sale on eBay? Maybe. Let's dive in and see how Best Offer works and why you may want to use it.

When you create a new product listing using the Fixed Price format, you will have the option to choose to allow Best Offers on your listing. If you check the Best Offer box, potential buyers will be able to send you offers on your products by clicking the Make Offer button on the product page.

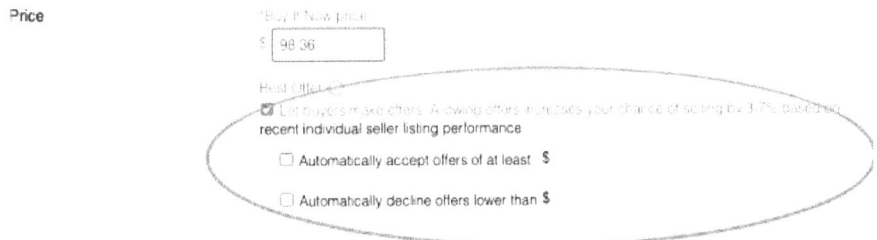

If you use the Best Offer option and have many listings, using the automation option allows you to set automatic decline and automatic accept amounts. The automation will save you a ton of time and keep you from dealing with the flood of low-ballers that think you will sell them your product for nothing. The automation options for Best Offer allow you to set a dollar amount that offers below that will be declined and an amount that any offer above will be accepted.

If you do want to negotiate with buyers yourself without using the Best Offer automation, I have some tips for you:

Why would you not use Best Offer automation? I sell high-dollar products, and I have had significant success in negotiating with buyers, even when they make ridiculous offers to start. If you automate your responses, you don't get the chance to communicate with potential buyers. If Best Offer works for you, don't miss the opportunity to convert offers to sales by negotiating skillfully.

New buyers often have no idea about how marketplace selling works, and depending upon what you are selling, they may not even know that you are a business that is reselling products. Let's educate them.

I use this messaging when I get an offer lower than I will accept:

Thanks for your Offer on PRODUCT X! I wish I could meet your price, but my cost is higher, and I have to account for the significant selling fees. I will counter-offer one more time to help as much as possible, but that is the best I can do. If we don't connect on this item, I hope we can work together in the future on another! Cheers!"

Here's the message that this phrase is sending and why it's so powerful:

- It thanks them and shows empathy – you want the buyer on your side.
- It informs them that you are a reseller with costs for your items.
- It helps to educate them about the significant selling fees sellers pay to eBay.
- It informs them that you will counter "one more time" – showing them that you are done negotiating.
- It is respectful and encourages them to come back to

buy something else in the future, even if you can't agree on a price for this item.

Sidebar: don't let your customers set your prices! You will continuously get low-ball offers for your items, especially in particular categories like fashion. Don't take it personally. Make your counter-offer statement and move on. Don't go back and forth, and remember that you control what your sale prices are.

I firmly believe that while you have to price your products competitively, you don't have to be the lowest price. You should focus more on providing epic customer service, incredible product listings, and building your credibility. Top Rated Sellers on eBay can always sell for more than regular sellers.

PHOTOGRAPHY FOR SELLING SUCCESS

You're ready to list your products for sale or improve your listings of items already for sale. We live in a visual world, and most potential buyers will NOT read your product descriptions and details, but they WILL look at your photos.

Let's start with the basics of product photography.

Lighting

Let there be light - LOTS of light! Many sellers have problems with getting the right amount of light focused on their products. Dark photos or photos with shadows are not going to help you make sales. If you are serious about selling, you'll want to set up a specific photo area with a solid white backdrop and artificial lighting to bring the bright to your pics. You don't need anything fancy for the backdrop - a bright white tablecloth or fabric (better than a sheet that you may see-through). Hang this backdrop from the wall and have it trail over whatever flat area you are taking photos on. You want a continuous flow of solid white. Of course, you can also buy a professional backdrop that will work great and offers additional options.

Background alert: you may be inclined to include a fancy background image or add accents to your product photos. Don't do it. eBay and search engine guidelines on photos consistently require a plain white background. Not only do plain white backgrounds make your products stand out, but search engines will only index product photos with plain white backgrounds. You want Google to index your listings on eBay since it will drive more traffic to your listings.

Say it with me now: plain white background only.

For lights, I recommend two or three bright, soft lightboxes like these that are available from eBay sellers and Amazon. You want to surround your product with light, eliminate shadows, and do your best to show your products' true colors. **I also recommend eliminating as much natural light as possible - you don't want reflections from windows or sunlight anywhere near your photo area.**

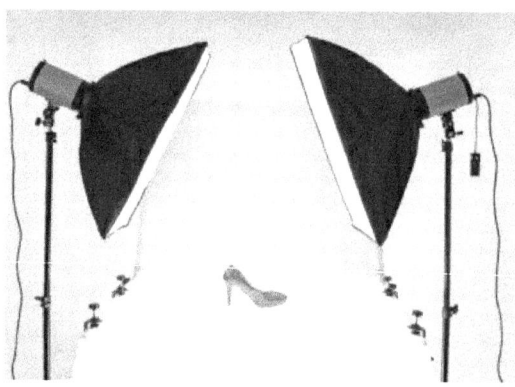

The Cover Shot

You only get ONE photo to capture users' attention when they are scrolling through a list of search results. Make sure your absolute best picture of your item is photo number one when uploading

Keep post-production to a minimum. One of the keys to success is the continual listing of products and interaction with eBay. By getting your photo setup figured out upfront, you'll save yourself tons of time by not having to edit or modify your product photos before uploading. Saving time becomes more critical as your business grows - you'll be busy making sales and won't have time to be editing. Of course, if you're only selling a few different products, you may need to edit to create the best photos.

Under promise and over deliver

I also like less editing because potential customers find non-edited photos more authentic, and heavily modified images can lead to disappointment when a customer gets the actual product. A light hand is best.

Stay away from filters or photo apps that make your products look different than they actually are. Focus (no pun intended!) on just taking great, non-edited photos and you will have happy customers.

The handbags that I sell come in all types of conditions:

- New, with tags – perfect condition
- New, with tags but with scuffs or damage from shipping and handling

- Gently used bags in like new condition
- Used bags with signs of wear.

When you are taking photos of these types of products, you want to **be sure to show any defects in your photos and to explain them in your product description.**

For example, in the photo below, I highlight a defect in the handle of a Prada handbag. You want to show these defects upfront, before a buyer purchases. You will avoid problems by being completely transparent about product condition at all times. You WILL still sell items with defects (and often make more profit doing so!), but you want to avoid having your buyers being surprised after their purchase.

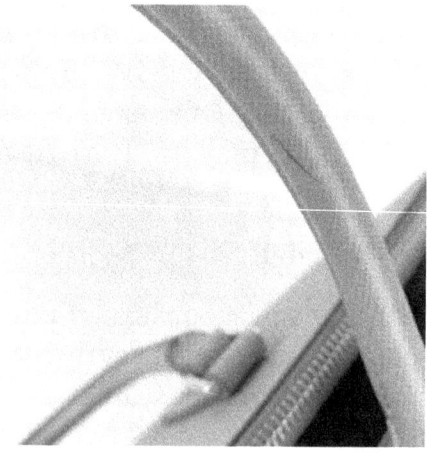

I love selling defective product! I pay less for it and I often make the most profit from these sales. I encourage you to think about defective or damaged items as a source of increased sales and profits.

Which Camera?

If speed is essential, using a high-quality smartphone like an iPhone with dual cameras (iPhone 7 Plus or newer) or Android device can work great. I find that focusing on production and getting new items listed beats out using a higher quality DLSR camera - but that's just my preference, and your workflow may work great with a DLSR camera. I like using my iPhone 12 because it instantly feeds the photos to the cloud for easy use when I am ready to list on eBay.

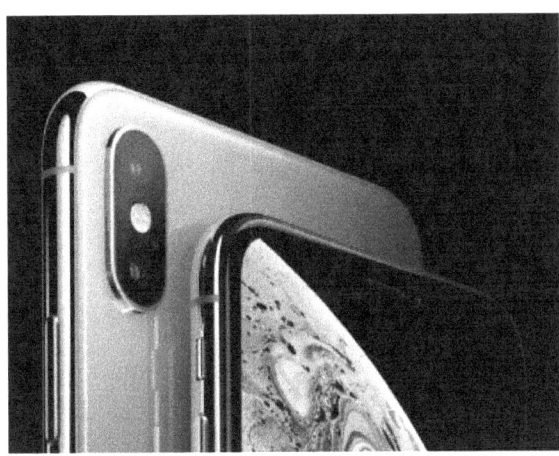

How Many Photos?

eBay currently has spots for up to 12 photos. I recommend taking as many photos as needed to show your product in detail. For my luxury handbag business, I take at least 12 and include photos of the inside of the bag, front, bag, angled, side, bottom, top, and model. Multiple photos are especially critical if you sell unique items or items that may have a flaw (like a pre-owned handbag). You want your buyer to see as accurate an image of the product as possible - including any defects or unique features. **The more you show, the less your returns will be due to expectations not being met.**

Need more than 12 photos?

If you feel you need more than 12 photos, use a photo combination App like Pic Stitch to combine photos into a collage that you can post as one photo. I use this for some of my higher-end Burberry bags that I want to show additional details like tag closeups, serial numbers, or "made in" tags.

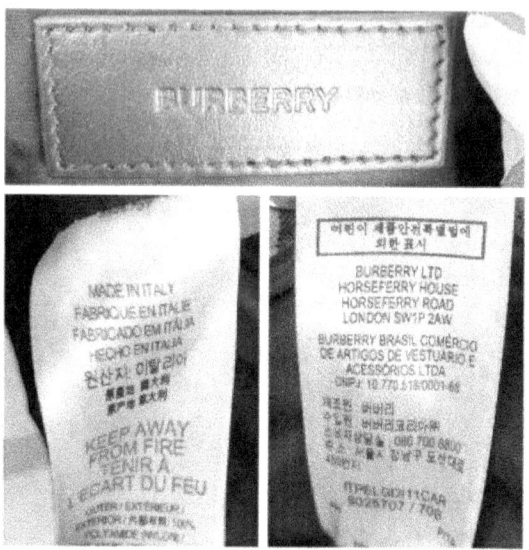

Using AE/AF Lock

If you are using a Smartphone to take photos, using the AE/AF lock can dramatically increase your pics' quality without having to edit them later. AE stands for Auto Exposure, and AF is Auto Focus. AE/AF adjusts when you take regular photos. However, when taking product photos, you may want to increase that light or change where the camera's focus is.

To lock and adjust AE/AF manually, simply press and hold on the screen while taking your photos - you'll see the AE/AF lockbox show up on the screen. Be sure to press and hold where you want the camera to focus. Once the AE/AF lockbox is on the screen, you can move your finger up to increase the brightness or down to lower. I use this quick edit often to bring out true colors and show fewer shadows.

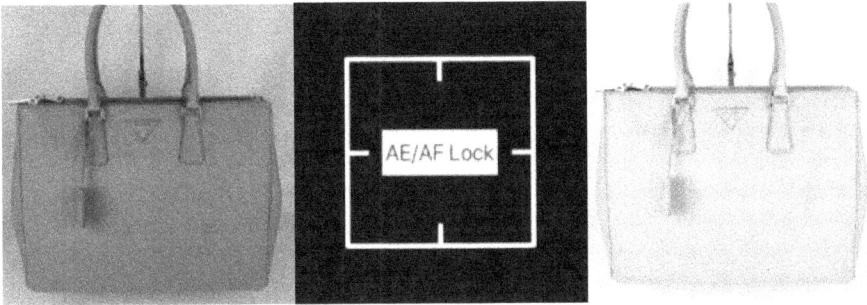

It's worth mentioning again that what we are doing here is try-ing to show the TRUEST image of the product you are selling. **We are not enhancing the photo to make the product look bet-ter than it is.** The AE/EF lock also shows true colors – as you can see from the handbag photo above, the photo on the right is much more accurate and shows the actual Prada Granito color that this bag is.

If you would like to learn more about using the AE/EF Lock to increase your photos' quality, the iPhone Photo School website has a great article with lots of tips.

Be a Square

Another Smartphone photo tip - use the Square photo setting on your phone's photo app to keep your product photos in the perspective that eBay likes best. If you have an iPhone, you also want to turn off the Live Photos option, which helps keep your photo storage from taking up too much space. In square mode, you'll also see less cropping when you upload images to eBay. Less cropping = fewer surprises and post-production re-sizing.

Change it up!

If you have a product listing that isn't selling well, try changing the cover photo – either with a different photo you are using on the listing or take an entirely new photo. Changing the cover photo can make a big difference for slow-selling stock. Trying new things is an essential strategy when items are not selling.

Workflow Tip

The first photo I take always contains the SKU/Product number I assign to the product I am listing. A SKU photo allows me to take a series of photos and then come back to organize and post them later. This first photo is for my internal tracking use only.

The first photo always shows SKU for my internal records of the next batch of pics

I then create a new record in my inventory database for each product when I am listing it. I use the SKU number to keep track of my cost, supplier name, and more. We will discuss inventory management, you guessed it, later in the book.

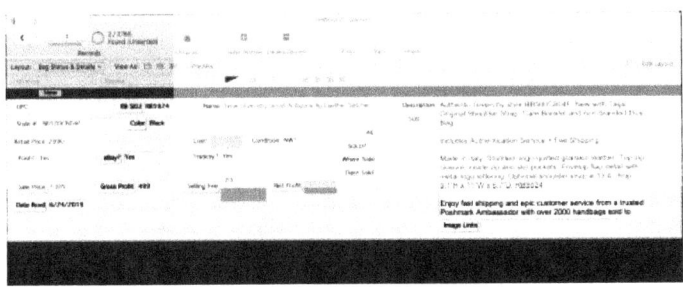

Revisiting the photo tips in this section:

- Use multiple lights to lose the shadows on your products
- Shut out natural light
- Use a white background
- Make your Cover Shot your best photo
- Use a Smart Phone with dual cameras if possible
- Maximize the number of photos you are taking
- Use AE/AF settings to show the actual condition and

color of your products

- Limit cropping by using the Square settings on your smartphone or other cameras.

PRE-SALE MESSAGING THAT CONVERT WATCHERS TO BUYERS

I attribute a large part of my success with online selling to how I communicate. I have learned over tens of thousands of transactions how to "talk" to potential buyers and customers via email and marketplace messaging that instills trust, credibility, empathy, and a bit of humor to the conversation.

This chapter will focus on pre-sale messaging, but you can also use the techniques here anytime you communicate with customers.

"I have a question..."

This type of message will fill up your email and eBay message list over and over. Customers want to know more, always. Even if you could answer every question with details in your product listings, most customers will never read it. It's easier to ask a question.

Many sellers are bothered by messages and see them as slowing down their productivity. I disagree. By using Text Automation and speedy response times, you can quickly increase your sales. Many customer questions are just a test to see if you will indeed respond. A quick, thorough, and friendly response can instantly convert a watcher into a buyer. Here's how I use eBay messaging to make more sales and build trust with potential buyers.

The need for speed

When a potential buyer sends you a message, they are actively SHOPPING. If you wait for 24-hours to reply to them, chances are they may no longer be shopping. Speed is essential if your item is not unique and there are many sellers on eBay. The question asked of you may have been sent to multiple sellers to see who would respond first. If you can, respond quickly to messages. Use the eBay App on your phone and embrace the concept of Text Automation (see that chapter for more details) to make short work of standard questions that you will get asked frequently.

Embracing Emojis

I know, I know. I held back for a long time from using Emojis in emails and messaging. However, studies show that a smiley face Emoji can instantly build a bridge to who you are communicating with. Consider adding an Emoji or two in your messaging – your customers will find it endearing, and it goes a long way towards connecting on a different level with your buyers.

Here's an example of a standard message I automatically send to every buyer:

Thanks for your order! I will ship the bag out quickly and send you the tracking number. I hope you love it! ❤◆◆◆◆

I am trying to share in the excitement they must be feeling when buying a handbag from me. My products are emotional purchases, and I am leaning on that to connect to my buyers.

Be excited!!

Here's something else I had to get used to when the only time I get to communicate with customers is via messaging. Using these!! Exclamation points are your friend. Remember, text is dry and dull (except when you add those so cool emojis I mentioned above). You want your customers to know that you are excited to help them and excited for them to buy from you.

Here's a sample of a message I use if I am negotiating with a customer:

Thanks for your offer on the XXX bag! I wish I could meet your price, but my cost is higher, and I have to account for the 20% selling fees. I will counter-offer one more time to help with shipping costs, but that is the best I can do. If we don't connect on this bag, I hope we can work together in the future on another! Cheers!

This little message has converted so many sales for me that I have lost count. I use it every-single-day. It's a quick text automation that works wonders to convert low-ball offers to full-priced sales. So, don't hold back. Be excited! ;-)

Automate Your Messaging

One of the best time-saving methods I use each day is the use of text expander apps. These apps allow me to save pieces of text or other media that I use repetitively when communicating with customers. If you are selling on your own web- site, marketplaces like Poshmark, eBay, Tradesy, and others, a good text expander app can save you a tremendous amount of time and energy.

Why do text automation apps make you more productive and help you offer better customer service? Read on!

Same Questions – Different Customers

I sell on several different marketplaces, and it's a great way to attract customers to your products or services. One problem is there is no place for you to create an FAQ document to answer common questions about what you're selling. Even if you did have a spot for an FAQ, do you think people will read it? Most will not – it's easier to ask a question than to dig through a list of answers.

With an automated text expander app on your desktop or smartphone, you can create answers to the questions you get asked over and over. These text snippets are saved on your device and recalled by typing just a few letters on your keyboard.

For example, one question I get asked multiple times each day is if I will sell a product at a lower price or accept a specific offer. My response looks like this:

I type: <u>pof</u>

And my text expander app instantly pastes this response to wherever my cursor is:

Hello! I am always willing to consider reasonable offers. Please use the Offer link to submit. Thanks!

This is a short one, but you could store an entire letter, batches of photos, or anything else you need to share over and over in your text expander app. For me, some common snippets are my shipping address, directions, links to various websites and marketplaces, dozens of answers to common customer questions, and much more.

Another example: I type <u>eof</u> and the text expander app types:

Hi!

I see that you are watching this handbag. Here's a discount offer that may help.

Please note that this offer is being sent to multiple potential buyers, so the bag is subject to being sold at any time.

Cheers!
Shannon

I have hundreds of these little text snippets saved on my computer and my iPhone. I respond to messages about a million times faster by using text automation apps instead of having to type out the same responses over and over.

Accurate – Every Time

Another benefit to using a text automation app is the consistency of the data that you are sharing. Create and proofread your text one time and then use it thousands of times in a snippet, and you'll always be sharing the correct address, contact info, product details, and anything else you use repetitively.

Stay on Message

Some text expansion apps allow you to share your text snippets across teams. This is a great way to ensure your employees or contractors are all on message – answering questions the same way and interacting with customers with the same in- formation. You get to set the tone and ensure that things are handled in the manner you want them to be. **These saved messages allow you to keep tight control over how customer issues are addressed, which can be especially important for new team members, which may not be experienced in handling**

questions, returns, or other customer service issues.

Now that we know a few main reasons you need to use auto-mated text apps, let's highlight a few apps for you to consider using.

TextExpander – Mac/Windows/iOS

This app changed my life, and it can change yours. TextEx-pander is the gold standard for text automation apps and is incredibly versatile when it comes to sharing snippets across all of your devices and with your entire team. You'll end a very reliable app with a tremendous depth of features and generous support from the TextExpander team. Setup as a subscription service so you don't need to keep paying for upgrades, you can save 20% off your first year by going to https://textexpander-.com/podcast when you signup. Please select The Small Business Show for the "where did you hear about us?" question in the pull-down menu.

Typeit4Me – Mac/iOS

A low-cost option that works great with Macs, iPhone, and iPad devices. A One-time fee of $19 gets you the desktop App. The interface is a little clunky but works for me once you get things set up.
https://ettoresoftware.store/mac-apps/typeit4me/

aText – Mac

Another low-cost Mac-only App that sells for $5. An excellent way to get started in the text expansion world with a reliable option for Mac users. You'll need to use DropBox or Google Drive to sync snippets across devices.

https://trankynam.com/atext/

Typinator – Mac

Another excellent text expansion App that works great for Mac users. Worth reviewing if you don't like any of the Apps listed above. https://www.ergonis.com/products/typinator/

Text automation can save you a tremendous amount of time and help you provide consistent messaging to your customers.

DON'T GET STUCK SELLING JUST ON PRICE

Everyone wants a great deal, and yes, most people are searching for the lowest price on an item if several different sellers are selling it. Your job is to use what you learn here and the knowledge you gain over time to convince potential buyers that there is more to a good purchase than just the lowest price.

It's important to know that there will always be someone or some company that can offer a similar or exact product for a lower price. This other seller may have gotten a great price on the item, they may be selling a product as a loss-leader to attract customers or some other reason that's not as important to the discussion. More importantly, we want to have a mindset that frees us from the trap of always being focused on price.

Don't get me wrong, you will have to be competitive to make

sales, but you don't have to, and you don't want to be the lowest priced when selling on eBay and other marketplaces.

Let's break this down and discuss what you can do to avoid having to compete just on price – which is a losing strategy in the long run.

Everything you are learning in eBay Unlocked and all of the knowledge you will gain as you begin making sales and working with customers will help you avoid the low-price trap.

1. Credibility and your Story – having a credible and trustworthy-looking product listing and a compelling story about you and your business. This builds trust and comfort for a buyer, and they are willing to pay more for it.

2. Having an established eBay Store – your store will help to build your brand and inspire confidence. Buyers will see that you are on eBay for the long run, and you are an established seller.

3. Generous return policy – this is a big one. 78% of customers surveyed have stated that they will pay more for a product on eBay if the seller has a 30-day return policy. Keep in mind that this does NOT generally increase returns, as I mentioned previously. Buyers just want to know that if something goes wrong, they can return an item. Sellers with no return policy do not inspire confidence.

4. Be yourself and be authentic – use conversational language in your listings and in your eBay messaging to connect with buyers on a different level. See the chapter on eBay Messaging for more info about this concept.

5. Take great photos – use the tips and techniques in the

photos chapter to present your products professionally.

6. Use Titles that inspire confidence – keywords such as
Authentic, New, Rare, Limited, and more will catch a
buyer's eye when scrolling through listings.

7. Use the odd price suffix concept described in the Random Pricing chapter to capture buyers' attention.

8. Don't forget your added value – often, buyers will ask
you to match another seller's price or point out lower
prices on the same product you are selling. When you
get inquires like this, always ask yourself, "Why don't
they just buy the product at the lower price?" These
customers want all the items listed above in items
1-7, AND they want you to be the lowest price. **Don't
fall for this trap.** The value you are adding to the product is worth more than these buyers want to pay. You
can't offer Tiffany service at Walmart prices.

9. Compare Apples to Apples – if you are doing pricing
research or a customer points out another seller offering your product for less, be sure to compare the
condition of the items being sold. Other sellers will
often discount products that are store returns, may
have blemishes, missing accessories, or have damaged
packaging. These may be good values, but if you are
selling a pristine, new-in-box product, there's a reason
why your price will be higher.

10. Do your research – if you know the real value of the
products you are selling, you will be more confident
turning down low-ball offers, and you will be likely
to fall for the low-price trap. Do your research and
only buy products you know that you can price competitively and generate a profit.

These factors combine to make you a better seller, offer better service to your customers, and sell your products for more. As I mentioned in the chapter on Increasing Your Average Sale Price, being the cheapest is a challenging way to make money. Why not find products that hold their value more or that may increase in value as they become scarce?

Think about this important concept while sourcing your products to resale and while doing your pricing researching using eBay and Terapeak.

CREDIBILITY, TRUST, AND AUTHENTICITY

How do you elevate your business above the lowest price race to the bottom, sell more, and make less mentality? Start by building trust, showing potential buyers that you are credible, and being authentic and transparent in your actions.

Let's break each of these down.

Trust – it's hard to build but powerful once you have it.

When a potential buyer feels like they can trust you and the marketplace you are selling on, you are halfway there to making a sale. How do you build trust when you only have a few minutes or less to capture a buyer's attention?

- Presentation – clear and concise titles and product descriptions with no typos or grammar errors
- Clear, high-resolution photos – see the Photography

section for tips
- Product details – provide all the data needed to make a buying decision. Color, dimensions, model numbers, style name,s, and more.
- Buyer friendly policies – 30-day returns, offering free returns

You can build **Credibility** by doing the following:

- Pricing your products competitively – you don't have to be the lowest price.
- Promoting your positive feedback and sales history in your product listings and your messages.
- Becoming a Top Rated seller
- Responding quickly to questions or offers
- Becoming rated by the BBB and other consumer agencies
- Having a Credibility Statement in your product listings and messages.

What's a Credibility Statement? It's a brief comment about your business that you can include in your product listings and messages. Here's what I use in my listings:

Enjoy fast shipping and epic customer service from a trusted Top-Rated seller with over 3000 handbags sold to date!

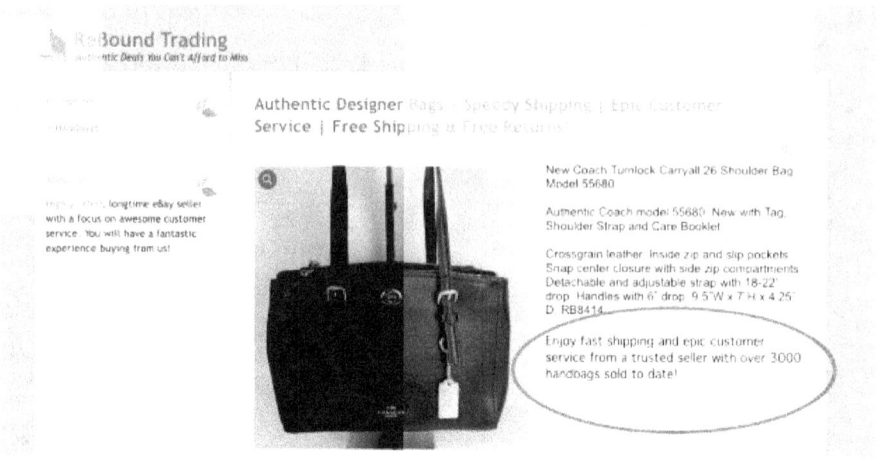

You can modify the statement for email or other messages. I answer questions for the potential buyer and then insert this statement:

Please check my sales history of over 3000 handbags sold to date and my feedback that has qualified me as a Top-Rated seller on eBay.

These statements are brief and to the point. They quickly tell a story that helps to build your credibility.

If you are a new seller, find something else you can promote about your credibility. Maybe you have a business that's been around for many years and are just starting on eBay. You could then use something like this:

Our small business has been operating for over 5-years with thousands of happy customers. We are excited to bring our products and incredible customer service to eBay.

You get the concept. Think about anything you can promote that potential buyers would like to hear about your business.

So how do you show your **Authenticity and Transparency**? Easy – just be yourself! If you are a small, one-person business, promote that aspect and mention how your customers get personalized attention that big companies can't match. If your company is enormous, talk about how you are super-fast or how your size gives you access to products at lower prices.

Don't try to be something you are not. Selling on eBay should be fun and rewarding. You will meet some great people, and as you learn about the marketplace, you will gain confidence in using the hundreds of different features and options.

If you are just getting started, share the excitement of this new adventure in your listings and with your customers when they message you. If this is a side hustle to pay for your kids' school, promote that! People love to hear stories, and you should share yours.
Be yourself when messaging with customers. If you make a mistake, own it, apologize and move on. If you don't know the answer to something, it's OK to say that and suggest that they search Google for the answer. There's no way you will ever have all the answers.

My advice is that it's better to be friendly and say you don't know something than to try and fake it. See the section on communication for more tips on this.

Credibility, Trust, Authenticity, and Transparency are what will make you stand out on eBay and beyond. These aspects are critically important, yet most sellers ignore them. Use this to your advantage, and you will thrive on eBay.

SELLING LESS AND MAKING MORE: INCREASE YOUR ASP.

Average Sale Price - these three words are critically important to your long term success on any marketplace, including Poshmark. **It can take the same amount of effort to sell a $10 item as it does to sell a $100 item.**

What can you do to increase your ASP?

Change your mindset: buying more and more since that is less work than selling will get you a massive death-pile of products that will drag you down mentally each time you look at it. It also ties up your cash and keeps you from investing in your business.

Fewer listings does not mean less profit: **don't get caught up**

with the myth that thousands of listings are required to have a profitable marketplace business. You can make more by selling less.

Research is King: spending time researching products and suppliers, making connections and building your network is just as crucial as buying products to resale. One new connection/supplier could change your life. Don't settle for the low hanging fruit.

Dump the dogs: get rid of products that don't sell. Keep proper accounting records and take the write-off for things that don't sell. Having your store/closet stuffed with slow movers hurts your sales of other items.

Good Data = Great Profits: keep track of what products, brands, and styles your customers buy from you. If your data shows that you don't make much money selling a particular brand, stop buying, even if their products are readily available.

The Riches are in the Niches: step outside and away from super competitive brands and product lines. These types of products are harder to buy, are usually more expensive and can have the lowest profit margin.

It's OK to start slow: finding higher ASP products can take time and effort. But it's no different than the time and effort to buy, photograph and list your low-dollar items. Use your time in a different manner that can have more profitable long-term results than listing the same types of low-dollar products over and over again.

Put the effort in now to create a system to research and make connections with the companies and brands you would like to sell. Use the LinkedIn system I have described in detail to build your network.

Lift your ASP and lift yourself!

CASH BACK MINDSET

Let's take a little breather from eBay-specific topics.

I want to take a few minutes to share what I call a Cash-Back Cost Method for reselling with you. This system is something that I have developed over time that has helped me tremendously by focusing on cash flow for my reselling businesses.

Here's how the Cash-Back Cost Method works.

Let's say I buy 50 products to resell, and my overall cost of those 50 products is $2000. If you use a cost per item method, you would divide up that $2000 50 times and come up with $40 per item as your cost basis. Over time, you record your profit based on that $40 cost.

In my business, however, this doesn't work that well. The reason is that there is always what I call the "cream" of the deal. These are the hot products in that group of 50 items that will sell the fastest and generate the most cash and profit. If I price every item at $40, I will be sitting on that $40 cash investment for a long time since I know some of those products just won't sell quickly.

My main focus is to get my initial $2000 back as quickly as possible with the Cash-Back Cost Method. I am always focused on cash flow since it is the lifeblood of my business. Without cash, I can't buy more products to sell, pay my bills, etc.

Out of those 50 products, I find the cream first, the most popular items that I can make the most profit from to generate the most cash. I put all my energy into selling those products first to get my $2000 investment back as quickly as possible. I may sell ten items for $200 each, and I have my $2000 back. What I do with those ten items is to "front-load" the cost of the entire purchase by listing the cost at $200 each for accounting purposes. I don't show any profit on these hot products, but I have recouped my investment of $2000, and I have 40 items left that have a $0 cost basis.

I then focus on selling those 40 items to book the actual profit from the $2000 investment. If I used the cost per item method, I would show a massive profit on those ten items: $200 - $40 cost. But I would be fooling myself since I would still have $1600 of cash tied up in the remaining 40 items that may sell slow or may never sell.

I look at my cash return each day from my sales. As the saying goes, my mind is on my money, and my money is on my mind. ☺

OK, let's get back to eBay specifics and talk about a topic I am crazy passionate about: Packaging!

PACKAGING – THE OUT OF BOX EXPERIENCE THAT WILL THRILL YOUR CUSTOMERS.

Congrats! You've made the sale, and you have a new customer. You also have a unique opportunity to make a long-term connection with your buyer to encourage repeat sales. **The way you manage the after-sale shipping, support, and follow-up are all excellent opportunities to show how great your business is and why your buyers should stay connected with you.**

The long-term value of your customer is exponentially more important than the one sale you just made. This section will focus on ways to impress your customers after the sale and make a long-term connection to bring you more business.

Let's start with the packaging. **If the first physical encounter that your customer has with you is your product arriving in a box to their home or office, it's critical to get it right.** Does your packaging impress or look distressed? What message is your packaging sending to your customer? When your box arrives, you have an opportunity to educate, bring a smile to their face, and build customer trust.

You worked hard. All your brand building and marketing has convinced a customer to buy your product. Your customer is eagerly awaiting the arrival of a UPS, FedEx, or USPS truck to drop off a box full of awesomeness.

What first impression will your packaging make to the customer before they even see your product?

It's just a box, right? WRONG – it's an opportunity

Your customer is waiting for your product to arrive. Whether you are a manufacturer or a reseller of products, after the purchase is complete and you or your team has shipped the order out, your customer judges you.

- Did they receive an order confirmation email?

- Did the order ship quickly?
- When the order shipped, did they receive a shipping confirmation email with a tracking number?

Each step of this journey is an opportunity to build trust and excitement with your customer. eBay handles the three items above for you, so you start strong.

Love at first sight?

What thoughts go through your customer's head when your box arrives? They see the outside of your packaging, and the judge inside their head returns:

- What condition is the box in?
- Is the box sealed completely?
- Is the shipping label on straight?
- Are their loose items banging around inside the box?
- If this is a high-dollar item, are tamper-proof tape or stickers intact?

At this point, you are still trying to build trust with your customer. Showing them you are professional and that you or your team took care to ensure that their order arrived quickly and in good condition. What may seem unimportant, like a straight shipping label, all add up to make an impression about you and your brand to your customer.

The Out of Box Experience

Your customer has your box and is impressed with how it looks on the outside. They grab a knife or razor and start to cut the tape. The court is back in session, and your customer has reprised their role as the judge.

Are vulnerable items directly below the cutting area that could be damaged when the box is cut open? If so, be sure to cover those items with something like a cardboard insert or packing paper.

The customer opens your box, and the first thing they see is?

A bunch of bubble wrap or other packaging filler? Information about how to process a return? How about a note from you or your staff? What about a photo of your smiling face or all of your happy employees together? Again, here's an opportunity to do something different and connect with your customer on an emotional level.

Even if you ship your products through a 3rd party logistics company or Amazon FBA, work on incorporating a Thank You note with each box – get creative – maybe the product box itself has the thank you on one side. Perhaps the thank you note is printed on the inside flap of the box.

Think about it – you are trying to connect with people that you want to come back and buy from you over and over. **Don't miss this opportunity.**

Solve problems and promote successes

The box is also a great place to promote quick solutions to common problems, provide support contact information, and explain how to process a return. Keep it simple and try adding a little humor to your notes – people react better when they know an actual human took the time to draft these notes.

If everything is fantastic, you want to encourage your customers to share the love and spread joy to their friends and family via whatever review platform you prefer or whatever social media you would like to promote.

I suggest offering some incentive for leaving the review or sharing their good experience. Something tangible that has some value. A favorite way to say thank you and keep engagement for my previous company, TechRestore, was offering double the warranty of a refurbished product if they left a review or signed up for our newsletter. Anything to promote a positive experience and to encourage them to keep in touch.

Box Different

NewEgg prints messages on their boxes in big, bold letters. Phrases like "May Contain Awesome" and "Exactly what you wanted. Guaranteed" help build excitement for the customer eagerly waiting for their product to arrive. These comments set the tone and connect with people on a much deeper level than just a plain brown box.

If you don't want to print a message on thousands of boxes, how about stickers with your messages that can be placed on packages as they go out?

Seth Godin wrote a book about standout marketing ideas titled Purple Cow. When you ordered the book, it arrived inside of a purple milk carton.

You get the idea. Put some thought and creativity into using your packaging to connect with your customers. Show them you are not just an average company, using the cheapest boxes you can find.

Don't miss the opportunity to send a message, make a statement, solve a problem, and connect with your customer on an emotional level. **Include your packaging and shipping boxes in your marketing strategy.**

SHIPPING AS A COMPETITIVE ADVANTAGE

We took a deep dive into product packaging and the "out of box" experience in the packaging chapter. I'm a bit obsessive about this topic, so I want to discuss some additional details about your shipments.

Customers are also obsessive about their shipments. You know how to create a great experience with your packaging, but there are a few more topics to discuss to help your eBay business succeed.

Speed – above all, customers want fast shipments. So does eBay. If you ship fast, your product listings will be promoted in Best Match search results. **If you say you are going to ship within 1-business day, do it**.

If you can't make that happen, just change your shipping settings to ship within 2-business days. It's better to under-promise and over-deliver than to disappoint your customers. eBay will also penalize you if you consistently miss your target ship-by dates.

You can set your handling time in the eBay Business Policy section:
https://www.bizpolicy.ebay.com/businesspolicy/manage

Welcome to business policies

I suggest you use the 1-day handling time option if you can. If you are following my concept of selling less and making more, your volume of shipments should be such that you can get orders out within 1-business day. If you need an extra day, that's fine. Just be sure to select the 2-business day handling time. Note that a business day is Monday-Friday, not counting weekends.

Tracking – most of you will be using the eBay built-in shipping options when shipping your orders to start. If you use the built-in eBay shipping service, your customer will automatically get an alert when you ship the item, along with an email that has the tracking information.

Tracking is critical to "prove" that you shipped the item. It can take 12-24 hours before a tracking number is active after you ship, especially during busy times of the year like the holidays. If you want your orders to track quickly, you will need to ensure that they are scanned by a USPS, UPS, or FedEx (depending on the shipping service that you use) representative when you drop them off. If you drop the orders into a drop box or have a pickup scheduled at your location, your shipments may take additional time to scan into the tracking system. This is OK, but you should understand how it works so you can explain it to customers when they ask.

Quality packaging – I believe you should be using new boxes with brand new internal packaging (paper or foam). This expense is well worth the presentation value when your customer receives their shipment. Here are some resources for you to get free or discounted pricing on boxes and fill:

USPS Free Packaging - If you are using USPS Priority Mail for shipments, there are some great free boxes currently offered. This packaging also ships to you for free. Here's the link to place your order for free shipping supplies: https://store.usps.com/store/results/free-shipping-supplies/shipping-supplies/_/N-alnx4jZ7d0v8v

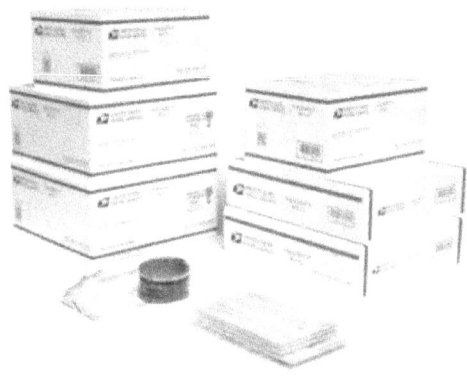

If you are reading eBay Unlocked as a printed book, simply go to USPS.com, click the Shop link at the top of the page, and then the Free Shipping supplies checkbox on the left side of the page.

You will also find free labels and stickers at USPS.com that are a valuable addition to your shipping supplies.

You may also need to purchase boxes to use for other shipping

services or different sizes not offered by USPS. If you subscribe to an eBay Store, you will get a $25 coupon to use on eBay branded Shipping Supplies each quarter. To get the coupon, go to https://www.sd.ebay.com/subscriberdiscounts

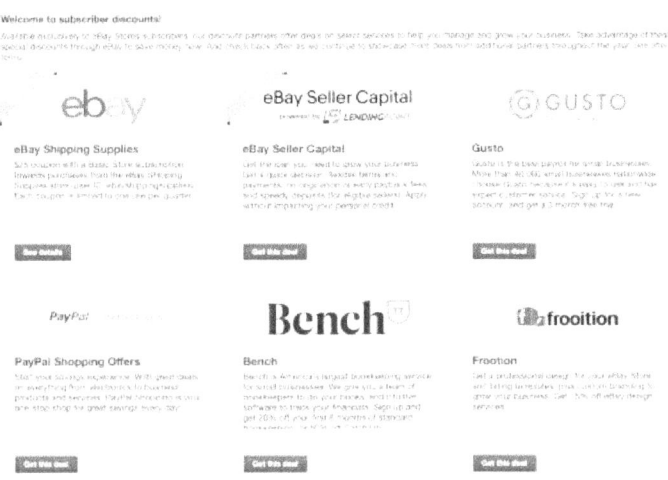

I also find good deals on other boxes by searching eBay as well as Amazon. I have found the best box sizes that work for me, and I use those dimensions to search on either marketplace. The same goes for other packaging supplies like mylar or padded envelopes.

Polybags:
https://www.ebay.com/itm/Poly-Mailers-Shipping-Bags-Enve-lopes-Packaging-Premium-2-5-Mil/313016663912

For inside packaging, I use foam and or crinkled paper fill. I purchase foam rolls on eBay from this seller that you may find helpful:
https://www.ebay.com/itm/1-32-PE-Foam-Wrap-Packaging-Rolls-24-X-2000-Per-Order-Ships-Free-/164640614201

For paper packaging, I buy from Zoro.com. If you subscribe to their newsletter, you will often get coupons for 20-30% off add-itional savings.

https://www.zoro.com/zoro-select-natural-kraft-paper-30-x-1200-ft-30-lb-basis-weight-5pgl6/i/G2397543/

INTERVIEW: ALEX KOEN, FOUNDER AND PRESIDENT AT CHRONOSTORE

One of the largest luxury watch sellers on eBay is Chronostore. Founder and President Alex Koen spoke to me about his success on eBay recently, and there's a lot to learn from the conversation.

Shannon: Alex, thanks for speaking to me today about your eBay

business. How long have you been selling on eBay?

Alex: Always good to talk with you. I am happy to help new eBay sellers. Chronostore has been selling on eBay since 2000.

Shannon: What categories does Chronostore sell in?

Alex: We sell in jewelry and watches, ladies handbags, and some cosmetics. We try to focus on luxury goods where the customer needs to trust the seller and is not just looking for the lowest price.

Shannon: Your sales volume is impressive, with over 3000 current listings on eBay. What is the most expensive item Chronostore has sold to date on eBay?

Alex: Our highest sale has been a Rolex watch for $75,000.

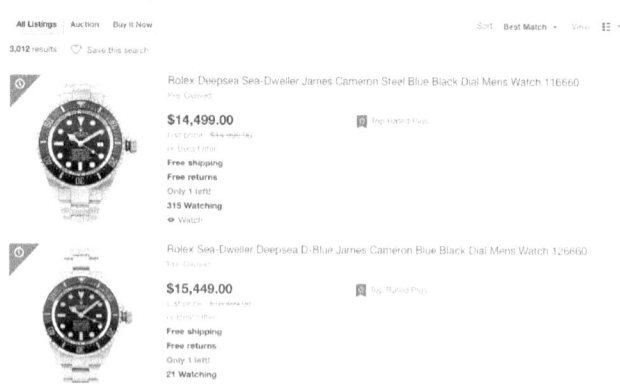

Shannon: That's awesome. How do you manage that volume of listings and sales on eBay?

Alex: We have some great employees, and we rely on automation software to manage everything. The primary application and service we use is M2E Pro. It is a lifesaver, and we could not live without it.

Shannon: Looking at the Chronostore feedback (over 10K left and 100% feedback!), I notice you accept a lot of Best Offers. Can you talk about how Best Offer has increased your sales?

Alex: Of course. Best Offer allows us to connect with potential buyers that usually would just keep scrolling to other listings. With Best Offer, they can see who we are and then connect with us with an offer. Many offers are too low, but we at least can begin the negotiating process. It is a bit more work, but as you can see from the feedback, we close a lot of sales with Best Offer.

FEEDBACK	FROM	WHEN
GREAT Item (MEN'S ROLEX)!!! JUST AS STATED Rolex Datejust 116203 SSJ Steel 18K Yellow Gold Silver Dial Automatic Mens Watch (#133480670089)	Buyer: d***m (1325★) US $9,099.00	Past month
Very happy safe delivery will buy again definitely Raymond Weil Tango 5399-STP-00995 Steel Quartz Ladies Watch (#133531348884)	Buyer: ***a (12★) US $371.07	Past month
Thank you for your business. A valued customer.	Seller: purchasedirect (6773★)	Past month
Beautiful watch! Fast shipping! Excellent transaction! Many thanks ☺ Bulova Stainless Steel Diamond Accented Dial Quartz Mens Watch 980001 (#154146130140)	Buyer: c***s (47★) US $157.37 (Best offer was accepted)	Past month
As described. Good deal Super fast shipping! Rolex Deepsea Sea-Dweller Steel Ceramic Black Dial Automatic Mens Watch 116660 (#154041305129)	Buyer: v***s (680★) US $10,899.00	Past month
Good seller ESQ Movado Two Tone Steel Gray Dial Quartz Mens Watch ES199 (#184108354738)	Buyer: 0***h (296★) US $138.57 (Best offer was accepted)	Past month
Exellcent to deal with, high quality, authentic, thank you so much for your help Authentic Cartier 11mm Black Leather Strap for Deployant Clasp 7DGBAC0 (#143767767343)	Buyer: l***_ (650★) US $190.00 (Best offer was accepted)	Past month
Excellent purchase Michael Kors Access Sofie Steel Rose Gold-Tone Ladies Smartwatch MKT5068 (#154269778181)	Buyer: a***t (131★) US $189.00	Past month
Watch is better than in the pictures. IWC Aquatimer Steel Chrono Black Dial Day Date Automatic Mens Watch IW376803 (#133585914927)	Buyer: e***_ (52★) US $4,277.07 (Best offer was accepted)	Past month
Awesome watch! Great seller. Great experience- Would buy again 😺😺😺 Hublot Big Bang Steel Titanium Rubber Automatic Black Mens Watch 301 SX 1170 RX (#143903498771)	Buyer: a***_ (121★) US $8,499.00 (Best offer was accepted)	Past month

Shannon: Did you start manually doing listings and then bring on software later as your business has grown?

Alex: Yes, we needed to learn how eBay worked in detail before we began growing our business.

Shannon: What's the biggest mistake you think new eBay sellers make?

Alex: I see it all the time. New eBay sellers often are focused just on being the best price. You will not be successful if all you are is the lowest price. That is a quick way to go out of business. Build your brand and your customer base over time with quality products and excellent customer service. That is the way.

Shannon: I agree. Sticking to the topic of mistakes, what do you think has been the biggest mistake you personally have made as an eBay seller?

Alex: My biggest mistake for many years was underestimating eBay staff's ability to help us grow. I did not think eBay was interested in Chronostore beyond just collecting the fees from our sales. But I have learned that the more we got connected with eBay, the more our business grew. eBay has really helped us as they have developed their watch authentication and guarantee program.

Shannon: What do you think eBay could do to improve their marketplace for sellers?

Alex: They are getting better, but there still needs to be more interaction between eBay management and sellers. Especially before the implementation of changes to the marketplace or new policies and programs. Long-time sellers need to be given a chance to provide feedback about how the changes or policies will impact their businesses.

Shannon: Do you think selling on eBay is a good way for everyone to make money or start a business?

Alex: I do, but that person needs to be self-motivated and have entrepreneurial skills. It is not hard to make a little money on eBay, but if you want to build a business over the long term, it does require business skills.

Shannon: Alex, thanks for providing some insight into your eBay experience, and cheers to your incredible success with Chronostore. If you could give one piece of advice for new eBay sellers, what would that be?

Alex: I would tell new sellers not to let negative experiences stop them. Be prepared for some negative things to happen but don't let that slow you down. Be persistent, keep learning, and you will succeed.

Connect with and learn more about Alex Koen and Chronostore:

LinkedIn:
https://www.linkedin.com/in/chronostorenyc/

eBay: https://www.ebay.com/str/chronostoreusa

Chronostore website: https://chronostore.com/

EBAY GLOBAL SHIPPING PROGRAM

The easiest way to sell your products internationally

Would you like to have a global reach for your products on eBay? Does the thought of dealing with customs paperwork and figuring out duties and VAT tax charges fill you with dread? Rejoice, eBay seller! The eBay Global Shipping Program (GSP) is your answer to a one-click method to offer your products to over 60-million eBay customers outside of the United States.

How the GSP works

The brief definition: Products you sell that qualify for the GSP are shipped to Kentucky, where an eBay service provider sorts packages by country and then delivers them outside the U.S. You are only responsible for getting the shipment to Kentucky. After that, eBay handles the rest. All of the paperwork, tax and duties collection if required, and more. You will get updates on the delivery progress, so you know when your customer received the order.

GSP is only available to sellers with an Above Standard seller rating or higher. Another incentive to keep your customer service skills strong. Since I know you will be Above Standard, let's focus on the GSP basics here, and I will provide additional links to take a deeper dive and sign up.

When international customers view your product listings, if you have signed up for the GSP they will see the final delivered cost to their location if you have signed up for the GSP. This will include whatever international shipping charges eBay calculates along with those pesky duties, taxes, and VAT charges. You won't see any of those charges come through your payments since eBay keeps them separate from the listing standard domestic charges.

Using the GSP, you will often have customers ask you for shipping discounts or to mark the customs paperwork as a "gift" so they can avoid being charged their countries fees. Since all of those charges are out of your control, you can simply reply that eBay adds those charges to your listing, and you have no way to change any international paperwork.

There are some limitations for GSP orders based on product value and weight. I think most of us avoid any weight issues since eBay's GSP weight limitations are very high, but the order value limitations typically have more impact. For example,

GSP orders to Russia are limited to $235 or less as of this writing.

You're protected

GSP users are also protected from negative and neutral feedback, and you can specify which products you want to offer for GSP. Just get your GSP order to Kentucky, and you're done! If the item is lost or broken during transit, you will still receive payment for the order as long as it arrived at the GSP facility in the U.S.

International Returns

You may want to create a different returns policy using the Business Policies section for international GSP orders. If you are offering free returns (which I think you should be), you probably don't want to offer free global returns, but that is up to you. You can also specify no returns or a shorter return window for your GSP orders.

Learn more

Here's the link to learn more about the Global Shipping Program. I ship orders via the GSP daily, and it has increased my sales by 11% on eBay. I highly recommend checking it out to see if it is a good fit for your business.

https://pages.ebay.com/seller-center/shipping/ebay-global-shipping-program.html

Get your account signed up for the Global Shipping Program. Go to:

Get your account signed up for the Global Shipping Program. Go to: Account > Site Preferences, then click the link to the right of the Shipping Preferences section. Click the Edit link next to the Offer the Global Shipping Program. Click on the opt IN button to sign up.

Alternatively, follow this link:

https://www.ebay.com/prf/GspOptIn

USING THE EBAY SHIPPING SYSTEM

eBay has a built-in system to ship your products out to your customers. You can choose to create shipping labels one at a time or in bulk. If you are shipping many of the same product orders, the bulk shipping method is a huge time-saver.

Let's jump into eBay shipping and see how it works.

Find the Orders Awaiting Shipment link in Seller Hub:

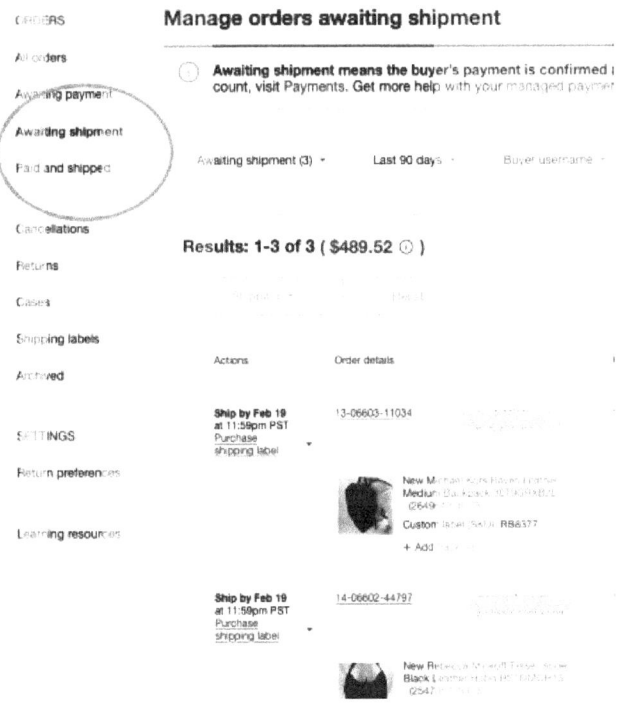

Decide if you wish to purchase and print shipping labels in bulk or individually. For bulk printing, click the Actions checkbox, then select Purchase Shipping label from the Shipping pull-down menu.

You can then enter weight and dimension information for your shipments.

If you are shipping individually, click the Purchase shipping label link next to each order. You will note that each order has a date to ship by to meet your business policies selection.

On the next screen, you will select which shipping service to use, enter the package weight and dimensions. eBay will provide a price for the shipment that you will be charged from your pending earnings or to your backup payment method of a credit card or bank account.

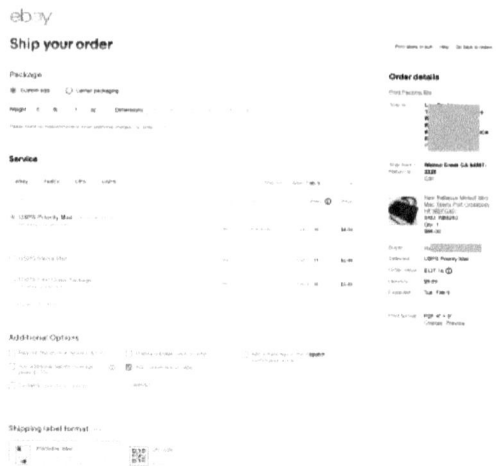

As I have mentioned throughout the book, there are many services and companies that provide eBay automation for tasks such as shipping, product listing, social media promotion, and more. A quick Google search will show you many resources to connect with those products and services.

We talk about automation and productivity frequently in the Unlocked Group for Resellers. Be sure to signup here: https://www.facebook.com/groups/poshmarkunlocked

EPIC CUSTOMER SERVICE

*The Two Tokens concept of
creating lifetime customers*

Mistakes happen. You will mess up, you or your employees will ship the wrong item out, a product will arrive damaged, and some customers are just not going to think you are as awesome as I know you are.

After 25-years of handling customers, I know that there is a right way and a wrong way to address these problems. I also know that a customer with their problem solved quickly and without hassles is extremely loyal and will spread the news far and wide about how great their experience was with your business. On the flip-side, information about bad experiences travels fast, and in the age of social networks, bad news can hurt your business for a long time.

Two Tokens

I didn't come up with this concept, but after reading about it a few years ago, I realized I had been practicing it and teaching my customer service team to practice it for decades. Jean-Louis

Gassée coined the Two Tokens phrase in an article he wrote back in 2017. Gassée is the former head of Apple Europe and a successful entrepreneur several times over.

The Two Tokens concept is that when a problem comes up with a customer, there are only Two Tokens that can be taken, and whoever takes the first one, the other person is forced to take the second. Let's unpack this.

Customer Jill calls or emails, and she is very upset about a problem with her order. Tom in your customer service department responds to Jill and takes a bit of a casual attitude about the situation. After all, it's just one order, and it's not that big of a deal, right?

Two Tokens are being played:

Token 1: It's Nothing

Token 2: It's Awful

Who is taking each Token? Jill is upset, but she had not taken a Token yet when she first contacted your business about the problem. Tom, on the other hand, has played the It's Nothing Token right at the start. Because there are only Two Tokens to play, Jill is forced to choose the It's Awful Token, and things typically go from bad to worse.

Jill responds with the It's Awful Token because she is angry that Tom is so laid back about the problem. This order is a big deal to Jill. Maybe it was a special gift, or perhaps she needed the item for a project on a timeline. Either way, Tom has lost the chance to control the situation and get on the same side of the table with the customer.
Let's look at the other option.

Customer Jill calls or emails, and she is very upset about a problem with her order. Tom understands the Two Tokens concept and knows what to do:

"I am so sorry about this situation! Rest assured that I will personally get this resolved quickly and to your satisfaction. Please allow me a bit of time to research this situation to come up with a solution for you. I will follow up within 24-hours. Thank you for bringing this to my attention, and again, my sincere apologies for this."

Tom has seized the **It's Awful Token** as he has been trained, and his response immediately calms down the upset customer because Jill knows that her problem is important to your company and that she is going to be taken care of.

IT DOES NOT MATTER IF THE CUSTOMER IS RIGHT OR WRONG AT THIS POINT.

With the customer calmed down and feeling like a priority, Tom can research the situation and develop some ideas about how to get things fixed. It could be that the customer is mistaken about something, or it could be that your company did make a mistake. Either way, Tom and the customer are now on the same side of the table, working TOGETHER to solve the problem.

When you show empathy, concern, and commiserate with the customer, you take the It's Awful Token away from the customer. The problem is put into a bit more perspective. The customer is almost compelled to think, "It's OK, it's really not that big of a deal."

What the customer really wants is to BE RECOGNIZED and taken seriously. Make sure that you and your customer service team always take the It's Awful Token first, and I guarantee that you will solve problems faster and create loyal fans of your business. Fans will share what excellent customer service they experienced when they bought from you.

AFTER-SALE TACTICS TO DELIGHT, YOUR CUSTOMERS

Congrats! You've made the sale, and you have a new customer. You also have a unique opportunity to make a long-term connection with your buyer to encourage repeat sales. **The way you manage the after-sale shipping, support, and follow-up are all excellent opportunities to show how fantastic your business is and why your buyers should stay connected with you.**

The long-term value of your customer is exponentially more important than the one sale you just made. This section will focus on ways to impress your customers after the sale and make a long-term connection to bring you more sales.

Follow up email

The good news is that once you make a sale, eBay is operating as your partner to keep your buyers informed about order status and more. The buyer will receive a confirmation of their order with projected delivery times based on the settings you are using from your Business Policies. When you ship the item, eBay will send a shipment confirmation to the buyer with tracking information. You can let eBay handle these for you, but I think there's room to improve on this.

If you are selling a high quantity of products, you may not have time to do this next step, but it can make a difference in your customers' feedback and overall mindset. I sell $10-20K worth of handbags on eBay each month. When I make a sale and receive payment, I always send this message to the buyer:

Thanks for your order! I will ship the bag out quickly and send you the tracking number. I hope you love it! ❤◆◆◆◆

I use a text expander app on my Mac and iPhone to make sending this quick and easy, but you could just as easily cut and paste the text from a note or word doc. This brief message has done more to build goodwill with my customers than you can imagine. It's just a simple message, but it stands out; it's not automated, and you are setting the tone of your relationship with the customer. If there's a problem with the order, you start on much better ground after the customer gets a message like this. Create your message or modify mine based on what products you are selling.

Thank you note inside your box.

See the packaging section for my slightly zealous take on why your box and packaging are crucial for your business. Right now, let's discuss the all-important thank you note.

Each order you ship should have a thank you note inside of it. You can pre-print these notes and have them inserted by your employees or your 3rd party logistics company if you are using an order fulfillment service. The thank-you note should contain:

A Photo: Your smiling face, a photo of your family, or a picture of your team of employees. At the very least, get a stock photo image of a happy couple of whatever face you want to put on your business. You want that personal connection.

A thank you: BIG letters – THANK YOU for your order!

Resources: Who should they contact with questions? Complaints? Praise? Reviews?

A reward: give them a coupon for a future order or for following you on social media or for signing up for your newsletter.

The goal here is to make a deeper connection with your customers. And again, if you don't want to use a photo of yourself, use a pic of your team together, or grab a stock photo that shows a smiling image of a happy person. **The key is to make an emotional impact with each of your customers.**

Thank you so much for your order!

We are here to help if there are any questions or problems.

Please message us on Facebook at the link below - We're here to help!

Let's be friends!
Visit us at facebook.com/reboundtrading

Thanks again!

Shannon & Renee Jean

Keep me! Mention this note for $10 off any regular priced bag in stock!

THANK YOU!

BUILD YOUR CUSTOMER LIST

When you sell on marketplaces like eBay, the customer belongs to eBay. This has many benefits, but one of the negatives is that it is more challenging to have a direct relationship with the customer over time. Here's where List Building comes in.

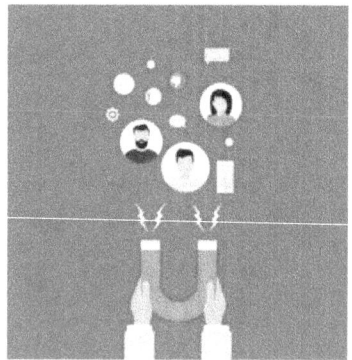

The call-to-action insert can be part of your thank you paperwork or on the 2nd insert inside your packaging. Here's your chance to connect beyond eBay.

Include a link to your website or the social network of choice. Entice your customers to follow you or to sign up for your list with a discount coupon for a future purchase or some other benefit. **Make it worthwhile for them to stay connected with you.** Be creative here.

You may want to include a 2nd insert inside each box, with more details about following your social accounts or joining your group. You can use phrases such as:

"Join my list of customers who get first chance at new product listings and get a discount on your next purchase!"

Or

"Get early alerts and exclusive discounted pricing by joining my customer list."

Stay away from words like "newsletter" or "email list." **Keep it personal and always focus on the benefits of joining this exclusive club.**

THE POWER OF SEARCH: KEYWORDS, SEO AND LIFETIME LISTINGS

I covered the concept of search terms and product descriptions in the chapter titled Your First Product Listing, but it is such an important concept, I want to take another dive and add some additional information to help you make more sales.

Do you browse when you shop online? When you are in the market to buy a specific something or other, are you randomly clicking around to view what a company has to offer? I didn't think so.

We shop via search. Either by entering terms or using filters and menu options to narrow down our choices. On marketplaces like eBay, over 70% of the sales start with a search. Search is paramount, and it impacts every aspect of your marketplace selling. Let's take a deep dive into search and learn how to maximize our product listings and our entire eBay account for search results both on and off eBay.

Search on the eBay marketplace.

When a customer searches eBay, the search includes your product title, your description, and those critical Item Specifics that I have been harping on and on about. Let's talk about your listing title first.

Your listing title is the first and often most critical text area for search results.

Keywords in your title: You have a limited amount of text (80-characters as of this writing), so you need to pack your title with the most relevant text and keywords that best describe your product. Here is what makes up a good title:

Product Type: handbag, pen, shoe, etc. You can use synonyms for product type, but you want to be sure you are not just stuffing the title with keywords. The title should read well and catch a reader's eye as they scroll through search results.

Product features Leather, Limited Edition, authentic, new, color, etc.

Example of a bad title:

Black leather handbag with liner

And a good title: Authentic New Prada Saffiano Lux Extra Large Zip Tote Model 1BA802

In this listing, I am telling the customer that:

This is an Authentic and New Prada

I list the handbag style: Saffiano Lux

I list the size: Extra Large

I list the Model: 1BA802

eBay says you don't have to list the condition in the title, but if I have room, I do it anyway since I think it catches the eye when scrolling through the search results. Now let's look at how to maximize your product description to show up more search results.

Product Description:

You should first know that many people will never see your product description. If they are using the eBay mobile app, they have to click a few levels down to read your description, and since we all know that people don't read, you will make lots of sales without customers reading your description.

Since that's the case, your Product Description should be brief and relevant. The description is not the place to stuff tons of extra text or "terms and conditions" that you expect people to read. They won't, and eBay sets the terms and conditions for their marketplace, and while you have many options, you have to follow their terms if you want to sell on eBay.

Here is what I like to include in the product description:

1. Restate the title. Just to be clear what you are selling.
2. I list the Model or Style number on a separate line
3. I show the Store Price. I don't use the term Retail Price since most people think the retail price is not real. Store price is the same thing, just a different way of stating it. Does it help? I don't know, but that's how I think.
4. I list the product condition specifics. This is the same as the Condition text that is below your title. Note that if your product is brand new with tags, eBay does

not show the Condition text area since your item should be perfect and brand new.

5. Product specifications. I list the dimensions, colors, and details that are important to the product I am selling.

6. I include my Credibility Statement so potential buyers know they can rely on me.

Here is what all that looks like:

I store all of this product information in my Sales Database. Be sure to read the chapter titled "Why You Need a Sales Database" for more info on this critical tool for your eBay business.

Now that you have your Title and Description setup let's revisit those pesky Item Specifics. Potential buyers are using filters and options to narrow down their searches. Those filters and options are directly tied to your Item Specifics and why you need to use as many Item Specifics as possible when creating your listings. Here's a snapshot of options available when I searched for Montblanc Pen on eBay:

Ink Color

- Black
- Blue
- Gold
- Green
- Multicolor
- Pink
- Red
- White

See all

Material

- Resin
- Gold
- Metal
- Silver
- Sterling Silver
- Plastic
- Titanium
- Leather

See all

Vintage

- No
- Yes
- Not Specified

See all

Features

- Chrome Trim
- Gold Trim
- Not Specified

See all

eBay is attempting to normalize and categorize millions and millions of product listings on their marketplace. Item Specifics is one of the ways they can get potential buyers to your listings faster.

Many categories have required Item Specifics. eBay will remind you when listing what is required and making suggestions about what additional Item Specifics would be helpful.

Best Match search results

eBay wants users of the marketplace to have a fantastic experience buying on their platform. One way they "tilt the scales," so to speak, is with Best Match search results.

Best Match provides search results that are not just based on what the buyer is searching for. Nor does Best Match always show the lowest-priced product listing first. Best Match is looking at the search query and then matching it with who eBay thinks can provide the customer's best shopping experience.

eBay makes the Best Match decision based on things like:

Your feedback ranking
Your sales velocity
How fast you answer messages from eBay shoppers
If you are a Top Rated seller
Have you had any complaints that didn't get resolved?
How fast do you ship your orders?
Do you offer free shipping?

All of this happens in milliseconds, and all of it impacts your success on eBay. I know it can look overwhelming for new eBay sellers, but trust me when I say that this stuff will happen naturally over time. You want to provide outstanding service to your customers. When you provide that excellent service, eBay notices and pushes your product listings higher in search results.

Best Match is critical to understand and one more reason you don't want to find yourself trapped in the "I have to sell at the lowest price" prison. There are many ways to sell for higher prices and to earn higher profits on eBay. Getting your product listings up higher in search is one way to create long-term, profitable eBay success. I am going to spend more time on the Low-Price Fallacy later in the book. It's going to be exciting, I promise.

Lifetime SEO

Before we leave the world of search, it's essential to understand two additional aspects and how it impacts your success. The first is Lifetime SEO, and the second is search results off of eBay.

What is Lifetime SEO? When you sell an item on eBay or if you cancel a product listing for some reason, the information does-not-go-away. Your product listing, all your hard work with your title and description, your incredible product photos, and more are kept on eBay and can come up in search results, over and over. This happens on eBay and search engines like Google, Bing, and DuckDuckGo.

This powerful concept is often overlooked by sellers, even though it can continue to drive sales to you for years. When you create your product listings, remember that the information may be shown to potential customers well beyond the lifespan of the product you are selling. Think of it as a living business card that can continue to send new customers to you. Be sure to create beautiful product listings with all of your business details so when those potential future customers land on a sold or ended listing, they will be impressed, and they will continue to find your active product listings.

Search Off eBay

Search off of eBay is another concept often missed. eBay spends billions of dollars each year with search engines to drive traffic to their marketplace. The more item specifics, the better product title, the more detailed descriptions you provide, the more apt you are to have your listings highlighted on Google, Bing, or DuckDuckGo. I encourage you to think beyond eBay when creating listings, when answering customer questions and when providing excellent after-sale customer service.

WHY YOU NEED AN EBAY STORE

Once you start listing your products for sale on eBay, I highly recommend subscribing to an eBay store. There are many benefits to signing up for an eBay store that I will go over below, but first and foremost, an eBay store is a fast and straightforward way to add credibility and trust to your selling account on eBay.

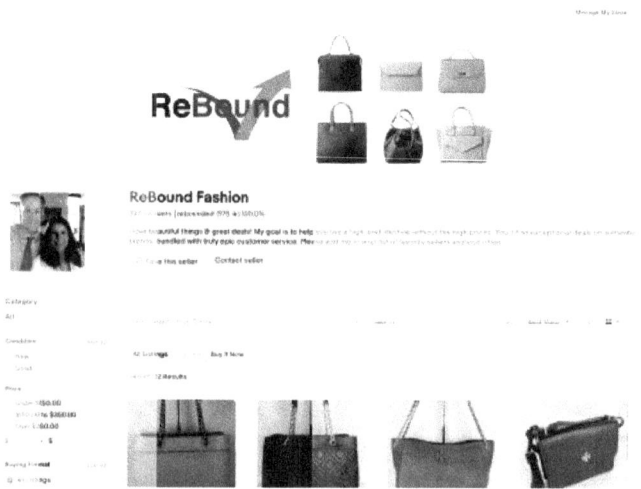

With an eBay store, you will have a centralized location and website address to highlight all of your eBay listings. You will instantly get access to better customer service as a store subscriber. Your customers will feel more comfortable buying from you as a member of the eBay store community.

Yes, you can and should still have your eCommerce website. If you have been selling products for any length of time, you probably already have a website selling products. The eBay store is an inexpensive addition to your eBay profile that brings many additional benefits. Such as:

A single URL (web address) to promote to other eBay shoppers where they can find all of your products showcased. Here's the link for my handbag eBay store: https://www.ebay.com/str/reboundtrading

Free listings: as of this writing, all eBay Store subscription levels qualify for 250 free fixed-price product listings and unlimited free auction-style listings.

Discount on final value fees – up to 60% off (depending on category) final value fees than non-store subscribers.

Access to eBay Promotion Manager – create discounts and promotions for your listings.

Access to eBay Markdown Manager – create markdown and sales events

Time Away – want to let customers place orders while you are on vacation and ship when you return? Get an eBay Store!

And more – see all the benefits here: https://pages.ebay.com/seller-center/run-your-store/why-get-an-ebay-store.html

eBay Store subscriptions start at around $5 per month for a starter plan and $22 for a Basic store. Compare the different subscription levels here: https://www.ebay.com/sub/subscriptions

Benefits

Insertion fee credits for auction-style items that sell					
Promotions Manager					
Markdown Manager					
Subscriber discounts					
Store home page	✓				
Link to eBay Store on listings	✓				
Listing frame	✓				
Selling Manager Pro	$5.99 /mo	$5.99 /mo			
Terapeak Research	$19.00 /mo				
Promoted Listings quarterly credit				$25.00	$75.00
Dedicated customer support					✓
10,000 fixed price listing allowance with zero insertion fee					$250.00 /mo
50,000 fixed price listing allowance with zero insertion fee					$1,500.00 /mo

Who it's for

Best for sellers who	List up to 100 items per month as either an auction or fixed price format	List at least 250 items per month as a fixed price format, or list high value items to take advantage of lower final value fees	List at least 1,000 items per month as a fixed price format	List at least 10,000 items per month as a fixed price format	List at least 100,000 items per month as a fixed price format
Eligibility	Have an eBay seller account	Have an eBay seller account	Have an eBay seller account	Have an eBay seller account	Have an eBay seller account

eBay store subscription prices look like this:

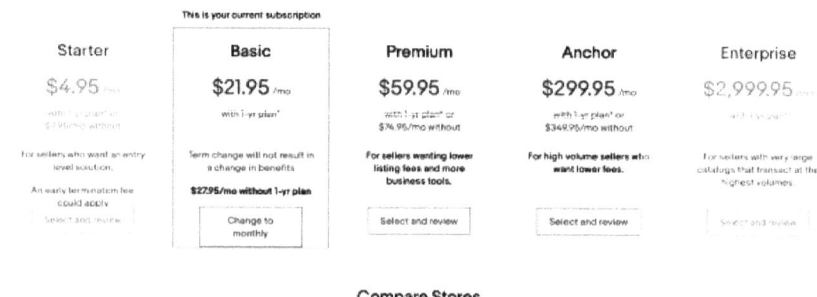

Choose a Store subscription

	Starter	**Basic** (This is your current subscription)	**Premium**	**Anchor**	**Enterprise**
Price	$4.95 /mo	$21.95 /mo	$59.95 /mo	$299.95 /mo	$2,999.95 /mo
	with 1-yr plan or $7.95/mo without	with 1-yr plan*	with 1-yr plan* or $74.95/mo without	with 1-yr plan* or $349.95/mo without	with 1-yr plan*
	For sellers who want an entry-level solution. An early termination fee could apply	Term change will not result in a change in benefits. $27.95/mo without 1-yr plan	For sellers wanting lower listing fees and more business tools.	For high volume sellers who want lower fees.	For sellers with very large catalogs that transact at the highest volumes.
	Select and review	Change to monthly	Select and review	Select and review	Select and review

Compare Stores

Find the Store that's right for you

	Starter	Basic	Premium	Anchor	Enterprise
Pricing					
Yearly subscription	$4.95	$21.95	$59.95	$299.95	$2,999.95
Monthly subscription	$7.95	$27.95	$74.95	$349.95	
Fees					
Free fixed price insertions	250 /mo	350 /mo	1,000 /mo	10,000 /mo	100,000 /mo
Free Auctions in Collectibles and Fashion	250 /mo	250 /mo	500 /mo	1,000 /mo	2,500 /mo
Additional fixed price insertion	$0.30	$0.25	$0.10	$0.05	$0.05
Additional auction insertion	$0.30	$0.25	$0.15	$0.10	$0.10
Final value fee	4.4 – 14.35%	3.9 – 14.35%	3.9 – 14.35%	3.9 – 14.35%	3.9 – 14.35%

Investing in an eBay store is a no-brainer, in my opinion. The benefits far outweigh the costs, and you can start small and scale up to a larger store as your business grows.

USING THE TERAPEAK RESEARCH TOOL

Terapeak is a free eBay research tool for eBay Store subscribers with at least a Basic store subscription. If you are a non-store subscriber or are using a Starter store, access to Terapeak is $12 per month for an annual subscription or $19 per month. Terapeak alone is worth the cost of the $22 per month Basic eBay Store subscription, in my opinion. Here's why:

Research best practices that bring in higher sale prices for the products you are selling. You will find the listings selling the quickest, getting more traffic, and selling for higher prices. You can then use those same best practices to drive more traffic to your listings and increase your sales.

You can also research supply and demand with Terapeak. Find out how many eBay users are searching for your product keywords and how much velocity is selling on eBay for a given period. This research is priceless when it comes to making buying decisions about what to sell on eBay. Using Terapeak, you can research sales, trends, and popularity BEFORE you buy to resale.

With Terapeak, you can analyze new categories to broaden

your product lines, see what your competitors are selling, what prices they are getting, and much more. Terapeak is a gold-mine of data and one of the only "real-world" analytics tools available to us mere mortals.

You will find Terapeak in the Research tab of Seller Hub:

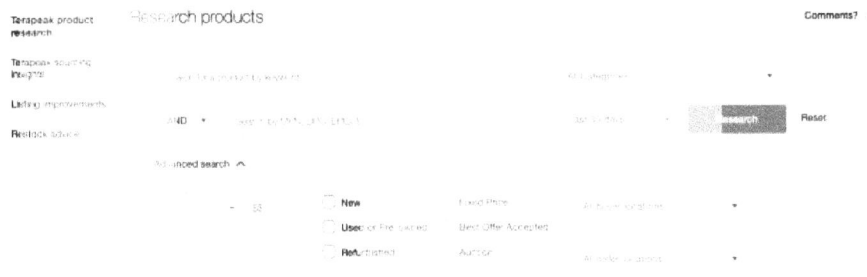

I did a sample search for Montblanc and got these results back:

Here you can see that Terapeak is returning the following data:

The average sale price of $165.25 with a massive sold price range of $0.99-$8500. This kind of result would require you to narrow down your search.

I changed the search from the generic Montblanc to Montblanc Starwalker black resin and got these results:

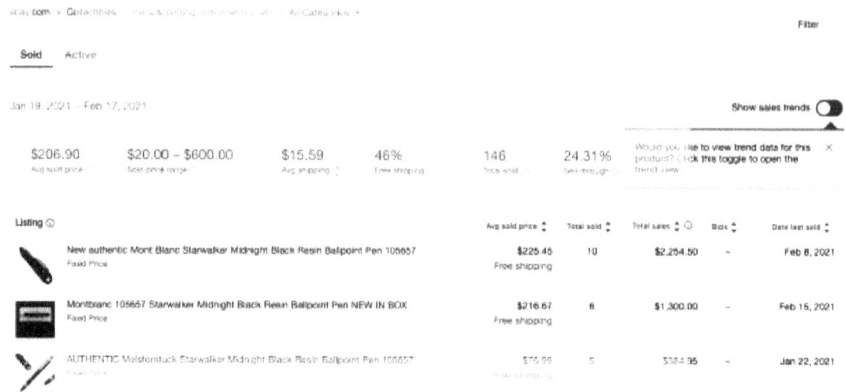

Much better! The average sold price is $206.90 with a range of $20-$600. You can also see the average shipping price is $15.59 and that 46% of sold listings included free shipping.

Terapeak also shows you the velocity of sales. Very important if you are researching what to buy. In this example, 146 units have sold in the past 28 days, with a sell-through rate of about 24%.

You can use dozens of other search parameters to narrow down the data that Terapeak shows you. I encourage you to experiment with Terapeak and use it as a tool for both selling AND buying. Just be sure to research BEFORE you buy.

THE BACKWARDS BUYING CONCEPT

Since we're on the topic of research, let's dive into a method that I use for purchasing products for resale: The Backwards Buying Concept.

How do you know if you can make money on what you are buying to resale on eBay?

That's a great question and a topic that should be on your mind. As the saying goes: Mind on your money and money on your mind! Here's a method that I use that has consistently helped me to decide if a product was worth buying to resale. I call it the Backwards Buying Concept.

When I am offered an opportunity to buy products to resale, **the first thing I do is make sure I know exactly what products I am being offered.** I ask for a detailed manifest of what is being sold. On this manifest (often a spreadsheet), I am looking for identifiers such as part numbers, UPC numbers, model numbers, manufacturer names, and descriptions, along with clarifying information such as condition, retail price, color, size, and more. The more information provided to you by the seller, the more likely you can research the real value of the products being offered to you.

Here's an example of what I consider to be a great manifest with enough information for you to do your pricing research:

Item Description	Qty	Retail	Condition	Model	Part #	Brand	UPC	Color
Note: These items are customer returns. Packaging and accessories may be missing or damaged. All products have been tested and found to be fully functional.								
TE15193011 MNS TED BAKER	21	179	A/B	TE15193011	TE15193011	Ted Baker		
METLCLTHRDALT31SHLDRBAG	6	395	C	79607	79607	Coach	193971368306	Black
37169 TORY BURCH PARKER	1	298	B	37169	37169-001	Tory Burch		Red

In this sample, you are getting some crucial information:

Line 2: The seller is telling you that these are customer returns, meaning that the product was sold and returned to the store by the customer. They may have changed their mind, maybe returning a gift or some other reason. Note that the seller is telling you that the packaging may be missing or damaged and that some accessories may be missing. Missing items are prevalent when buying store returns and should be calculated into the product's value when purchasing.

Line 3: If you are buying products such as electronics, watches, computers, or other products that perform a specific function, the seller is telling you that they have tested these products and found them each to be functional. Of course, tested products should have a higher value than untested store returns. New buyers should be cautious before purchasing any untested, as-is products.

Line 5: Description, Quantity, Retail Price, Condition, Model, Part #, Brand, UPC, and Color. All product details will help you come up with a price you can pay for this product and still make a profit.

If you get a manifest that only has a generic description like this:

2 Pallets of various customer returns electronics, tools, household goods.

Run away! Unless you are a very experienced seller that has experience with this type of as-is, untested, and un-manifested products, I highly recommend you stay away from these types of "opportunities."

Another aspect to always be concerned about is being rushed for time when purchasing. If you are contacted about a "great deal" that is only available today, and you don't have the time to do your research on the products, you should pass on that deal. Unless it's being offered to you by a trusted supplier, you already have a relationship with, and for products, you already know the market for, the rushed for time scam is usually too good to be true. Unscrupulous sellers are looking to make a quick profit from a naïve buyer.

So, you have an excellent manifest, and you do your product research to find out what the products are selling for. Remember, you want to find the SOLD prices, not advertised prices. See the chapter on eBay research for more info.

What I like to do when purchasing products to resale is to base my research on the lowest sold price I can find for the same condition product. I then work my offer on the products "backward" by taking the lowest price sold and deducting the selling fees (typically 15-20% on eBay) to get the net sale proceeds that a seller would receive when selling a product.

Let's take one of those products from the Sample Manifest image in this chapter:

Tory Burch Parker Tote, model 37169, Red, Condition: B

I find on eBay that this exact model Tory Burch Tote has sold recently for these prices:

$265
$240
$150

$235

I throw out the lowest price outlier of $150 and come up with an average sold price of $246.

$246 – Selling Fees (20% in this example) = $197 gross profit

I then ask myself what Net Profit I need to make on this Tory Burch Tote to make it worthwhile to purchase. I decide that I want to make a Net Profit of $50. If there are no other costs involved (shipping charges, for example), here's what I can offer to the supplier for this product:

$197 - $50 = $147

Make sense? I simply work the deal backward on each product. I have used this method for 25 years to buy tens of millions of dollars worth of products to resale. Everything from cranes to computers to iPhones, watches to handbags. It's a simple method that works because it's so simple.

A note about not winning deals. Maybe the supplier wants $175 for that Tory Burch Tote. Are you going to be able to run your business only making a $22 profit on that item? Only you can know that. Some companies sell large quantities of products that would be thrilled to net a $22 profit x thousands of sales.

My concept is different: less work, more profit, higher Average Sale Prices. This means that I pass on many "deals" that come my way, but I pick and choose the most profitable and focus on higher profit products that I can sell less of. The Backwards Buying Concept has worked great for me, but your mileage may vary. The key is to experiment and keep trying new things. You will find the method that works the best for your unique situation.

INTERVIEW: BUCKEY TURK

Founder and President at
Mac-Resource Computers
and Royal Warehouse

Longtime entrepreneur and multiple business owner Buckey Turk has sold everything from supercomputers to lincoln logs. He has created, and sold companies, employed hundreds of people, and been a recognized leader in his community.

Shannon: Buckey, thanks for talking to me today about your eBay experience!

Buckey: No problem. I always enjoy talking about business, and I have done a lot of buying and selling on eBay over the years.

Shannon: How long have you been selling on eBay?

Buckey: I started all the way back in November of 1999. eBay has grown right along with my businesses, it seems.

Shannon: That's awesome. What categories have you had the most success selling in?

Buckey: We mostly sold in the Computers and technology, vintage collectibles, and memorabilia categories, but I have experimented with all kinds of different categories.

Shannon: Have you focused on high-end products with big profit margins, or did you sell more high-volume, lower-priced goods?

Buckey: We did both. I sold truckloads of Apple computer products on eBay with some prices up around $2500 and thousands of lower-priced products. It just depended on what products we were involved in. We might be selling an entire computer system or just repair parts for those systems.

Shannon: Let's talk about mistakes since we all learn so much from them. Is there a common mistake you see eBay sellers making when trying to sell?

Buckey: Yes, and it's two sides of the same coin: too much information or not enough on their product listings. Many sellers list volumes of details in their product descriptions that not many people are going to take the time to read. On the flip-side, many sellers leave out critical specifications that are needed when making a buying decision. For example, today, I was looking for a gas tank for a generator I won, and most of the sellers list the size of the tank but not the measurements between the mounting holes to see if it would fit. I was ready to buy, but could not without those details.

Shannon: That makes sense. I always joke that nobody reads, but you still need enough specifications to make a sale. How about yourself, is there a mistake you have made that cost you in the long run?

Buckey: You bet. I would often assume that the customer would be able to figure things out on their own, without needing any support to make a purchase. But I have learned that doesn't usually happen. You have to have some sort of customer service in place if you want to be successful on eBay, especially if you are selling technical products.

Shannon: I know you sold Mac-Resource a few years ago, and I'll bet you're happy not to be dealing with those tech support issues anymore. Did you use any non-eBay software to manage your eBay sales?

Buckey: I don't miss tech support! For software, nothing for selling, but I used Bid Sniper to buy products all the time. I wouldn't buy without it.

Shannon: Can you tell us more about Bid Sniper?

Buckey: Sure. It's just a service that will place a bid automatically for you in the last few seconds of an auction closing on eBay. If you are trying to get the best deal on a product to resale or for yourself, Bid Sniper is the way to go.

Shannon: Do you think selling on eBay is a good way for everyone to make extra money and start a business?

Buckey: It's not easy. Just like regular business, you have to pay attention to detail, ship on time, provide good service and product. Just like any business, you need to separate yourself from the crowd.

Shannon: Good points! Thanks for sharing your eBay experience with readers of eBay Unlocked. If you had one piece of advice you could give to new eBay sellers, what would that be?

Buckey: Work your butt off, pay attention to detail, and do NOT neglect problems. It's not rocket science, but it's also not the easiest thing in the world.

To learn more about Buckey and Royal Warehouse, visit:

https://royalwarehouse.net

SOURCING PRODUCTS TO RESALE ON EBAY AND OTHER MARKETPLACES

Where are the best places to buy products to resale on eBay and other marketplaces?

How much do you need to buy to make enough net-profit each month to make it worth your time and create a successful small business selling on these platforms?

What products sell best on each marketplace and how do you figure out what you can pay for these products, and how do you decide on resale prices?

These are great questions! I get asked these every day as I talk to sellers and help Small Businesses find their niche on marketplaces. Let's break things down into three different sections:

1. Where to buy: how to find sources and connect with suppliers
2. How much do you need to buy to be successful?
3. How do you figure out what you can pay and how to set sale prices

Where to Buy, but first

Before we jump into how to find sources for products to resale,

I believe strongly that you first need to ask yourself this question:

What do I want to sell?

Do you care what you sell, or are you just looking to find anything you can get at a reasonable price and resale for a profit?

I would suggest that you have more success by narrowing down your target market and finding a niche that you can dig deep into, become an expert, and develop sources.

Finding sources and developing relationships takes time. It is not easy, and you will have to be persistent. Even though I had been selling on eBay for almost two decades, I owned companies that were primarily selling consumer electronics and computer products during that time. I sold the last of these companies in 2016, and I had to find a new niche that I could focus on as a solopreneur since I wanted to stay active on eBay.

I used other marketplaces and research tools to decide that Handbags would be the right niche for me. I know absolutely nothing about fashion, so I had to pick a narrow product category that my lack of fashion knowledge would not hold me back. I then spent months developing relationships with suppliers before offering my first product for sale. A few years later, I am on track to sell $750K worth of handbags this year.

The takeaway: Put as much effort into researching WHAT to sell as you do finding where to buy.

Where to Buy, but second

I promise I will get to tips on finding sources, but I want to spend a little more time on the background so you can increase the likelihood of success when you do find the right supplier.

I am an opportunistic buyer. I am always looking for deals in my product category, always looking for new suppliers and new opportunities. After studying the marketplaces where I would be selling, I knew that handbag designers and manufacturers would not want to sell to me directly. These companies typically don't want their brands sold on marketplaces, and even if they did sell to me directly, the prices they would offer would never work in these secondary markets. I would have to price my items well below retail stores or outlets to get any attention. I would have to try a different tactic to find inventory: overstock, end of the season, floor samples, and store returns.

Let's break down these three categories:

> 1. Overstock: a product that did not sell in the stores and is leftover stock
> 2. End of Season: as the seasons' change, so do styles, and here is your opportunity
> 3. Floor Samples: retailers don't like to have one of any item left on their shelves
> 4. Store Returns: retailers, distributors, and even manufacturers often have liberal returns policies.

Be a Problem Solver

One common trait that these four product types have is that they are all PROBLEMS for whoever has the inventory. Your job is to SOLVE these problems and to present yourself as a problem solver to the supplier.

It will be much easier to get a supplier to pay attention to you when you frame the discussion to solve a problem for them. Remember, everyone wants to buy the best brands, in perfect condition, at low prices. These suppliers get approached over and over by people who are looking for those deals.

In my experience, if you can approach a potential supplier and frame your request as "I can help you solve this problem," your chances of getting heard are much higher.

A caveat here: You may not make any money when you first start buying from a new supplier.

What?! That's right, you may need to pay more than others to get their attention, and you may need to help them by taking some slow-moving inventory off their hands. I call this "tuition," and it is always worth paying to get yourself educated and connected to the right suppliers.

Once you have a buying relationship, it will be much easier to get your hands on those great deals on perfect products. You need to prove yourself a bit, build up your credibility, and show that you are a problem solver interested in the long term.

Now that you have done your research about WHAT to buy and have some tips on HOW to approach suppliers let's discuss some ways to find them.

Product sourcing is the holy-grail of reselling on marketplaces. I am going to describe a few different methods to connect with suppliers. Most resellers usually ignore this first technique since it takes time, but it can yield incredible results.

Let's talk about LinkedIn.

Step 1: Go to LinkedIn.com and create a new account. Stop reading and take a moment to do it now. It's quick and easy. You'll want an account so you can set up your profile as you read along in this section.

LinkedIn account created? Great!

Step 2: Connect with me. Go to my LinkedIn page via the link below and click on the Connect button. You will then have an option to send a personal message along with your connection request. ALWAYS send a brief message when you are making new connections. Click the Add a note button.

https://www.linkedin.com/in/shannonjjean/

Shannon Jean
Founder | Advisor | Author | Fishing Buddy
Lafayette, California, United States · 500+ connections ·
Contact info

The Small Business Show

Send me a message – something along the lines of "Hi Shannon – I am reading eBay Unlocked, and I am learning about using LinkedIn to connect with suppliers. I would like to add you to my network. Thanks!"

This message is relevant, brief and it gives me a reason to connect with you. Keep this in mind since you will be creating similar messages when you connect with other LinkedIn members.

Here's is what I suggest you do next to complete your LinkedIn profile:

On your LinkedIn profile, you want to represent yourself as your business entity. List yourself as Founder, President, Manager – whatever you like, but give yourself a title and explain what you do in the About section. You don't need to mention where you sell your products. Here's an example:

Jerri Shoe – Founder, Brilliant Shoes
Brilliant Shoes provides exceptional value and a wide array of brands of casual, professional, and sports shoes. I am continuously on the lookout for great deals to pass on to our customers. We buy overstock, end of life, and job-out inventory. We are problem solvers!

You get the idea. If you want to build a business, be sure you look like a business. Begin connecting with anyone else you know on LinkedIn. Friends, business associates – anyone. Start to build your network with people you already know.

Note that some higher profile members will not have a "Connect" option. You will often see a Follow button in place of Connect. Go ahead, follow these superstars. I will show you how to connect with them in other ways.

Next, think about the products you want to sell. If you are into shoes, start searching for shoe brands you are interested in. Connect with people that work for Nike, Adidas, etc. Also, think about stores that sell shoes and start connecting with people who work for stores that sell the brands you want to sell.

Use the search feature on LinkedIn to find people in the industry you want to source products from. Create a standard message to connect with them – something like this:

Hi <Macys executive>

I would love to add you to my network. I am a shoe reseller that is passionate about problem-solving for my suppliers. Cheers!

If that message doesn't work for you, change it up – try different ones to see what type of narrative works best to make connections. You always want to be telling your story.

Once you have some connections, you will begin to see posts and comments from these potential suppliers in your LinkedIn news feed. Make comments on these posts – thank them for sharing the info, congratulate them for their successes, etc. Interact as much as you can.

10-20 minutes per day on LinkedIn can dramatically increase your long-term success as a reseller. Why? Because you want to build up a history with deep connections. I spent nine months using this method to connect with handbag companies, distributors, and retailers when I finally made a connection that instantly brought truckloads of products to me at incredible prices. This process works!

Once you have some connections, think about the problems

they face and how you could solve them. My opening question has always been: "Sell me your problem inventory" – stuff that hasn't sold, returns, end of the season – whatever.

If you can solve a problem, you will be able to build on those connections. I started by literally buying their junk – terrible condition products that no one else wanted to buy. Most buyers just want the buy the best product at the lowest price – THIS DOES NOT WORK. You want to focus on solving those problems.

Always be a problem solver. I have heard suppliers tell me directly that the reason they began selling to me was that I was not trying to "cherry-pick" and buy only in-demand products at low prices. I invested a significant amount of money buying handbags that I would eventually donate or sell at cost – just to prove to these suppliers that I could be a valuable resource for them.

Now let's really turn things on their head and talk about using eBay to find suppliers. Yes, the same place you will be selling! Finding suppliers on eBay can dramatically help expand your list of suppliers for your resale business.

First, why is it important to always be adding new suppliers?

1. It makes your business more resilient – not being reliant on a small number of suppliers.

2. You will learn more – new product lines that may be more profitable than the products you are currently selling.

3. New connections can be life-changing – one new supplier can completely change your business or introduce you to another person to help you tremendously. Don't underestimate the power of a robust network.

How will we use eBay to find these suppliers and make our life much better? Let's find out.

Familiarize yourself with eBay

You want to spend time on eBay to learn about the marketplace. The more familiar you are with listings, options, search techniques, and the marketplace in general, the easier it will be for you to find success. I prefer the web-based version of eBay vs. the App since it gives you more options for search, and information is just presented in an easier-to-use format.

Capture data

I will share some search tips in this article, and you will want to capture the data you find, data such as user names of sellers you want to research more. You should have some sort of database or spreadsheet where you can keep the information you find. The more data you collect, the more powerful a resource eBay can be for you over time.

Recognizing patterns

With the data you are capturing and saving, you will find the names of the sellers that are generating the most revenue in the categories or specific products you are targeting. You are looking for consistent information that you can use to connect with high-volume sellers on eBay to connect with and possibly convert to a supplier for your business.

Don't buy from end-users

Once you begin to recognize and capture seller information, you will quickly identify end-user sellers selling their items vs. pro sellers running a business on eBay. I highly recommend you stay away from end-users. When buying from end-users, you are just not going to create a consistent experience that is repeatable for your business. You will also open yourself up to issues with authenticity, product condition, and poor customer service that you can overcome when buying from a pro seller.

Find the Top Sellers – how to locate pro

sellers in your categories.

Search for the products you are interested in sourcing for resale, and then check the boxes on the left of your screen to show only SOLD listings. This will change the search results to show only sold items. Click into listings that look professionally created – you will quickly learn how to discern these pro listings – often new products, better photographs, well-written titles.

Hunter Women's Original Short Gloss Navy Rain Boots Size 9 B(M) US See original listing

Condition:	New with box
Ended:	Jun 29, 2020, 8:55AM
Price:	US $80.00 [1 sold]
Shipping:	FREE Standard Shipping
Item location:	Hempstead, New York, United States
Seller:	meit.us2015 (8691 ★) Seller's other items

Sell one like this

Once you click into a particular listing, check the feedback number for the seller. You want sellers with a large number of feedback results that will indicate that they are volume sellers. Click the seller's other items link to see a list of items for sale and confirm that they are a volume seller.

How to contact.

Keep a list of these reseller account names in your database or spreadsheet. You want to be able to track the date you contacted them and any responses from them.
To start the contact process, click on the seller name from any of their product listings. Then find the Contact link at the top of the page. Check the box on the contact page that reads, "This is not about an item," and create your message.

The message matters.

You are fishing here – start your fishing expedition in very general terms to see if the seller is interested in speaking to you about wholesale sales. Here are some examples of the messages that have worked for me in the past. I never give up after only one message; I use a 3-step process of being patient, consistent, and polite:

Message 1:
Hello!
I am a new seller, and I see you have a successful business here on eBay. Would you be interested in selling wholesale quantity lots? My interest is not to compete with you but to expand onto other marketplaces. Thanks for your time, and I hope to connect with you soon.
-Your name-

Message 2 (no response follow up):
Hey there!
I sent a message last week about purchasing quantity items that you have for sale. I am sure you are busy, so I'll keep it short. Would it be possible to buy wholesale quantity lots from your business? Please let me know either way and thanks for your time!
-Your name-

Message 3 (no response 2nd follow up)
Hi,
I just wanted to reach out one more time to see if there was any possibility that I could buy in quantity from you. I am very flexible about how it could work and be sure not to compete with your business on eBay. Thanks again, and I hope to hear from you soon.
-Your name-

Of course, you should edit these messages as you wish to make them work for your needs. The key for me is consistency, giving them 3-5 days before sending the 2nd and 3rd messages, and always being polite. Each time you send Message 1, 2, or 3, record it on your spreadsheet so you can remember where you are at in this supplier recruitment process.

Off-marketplace purchases

Ultimately you want to make your wholesale purchase off eBay, so the seller avoids selling fees, and you can get better pricing. Of course, eBay doesn't like this, so you want the seller first to make this suggestion, if possible. Ideally, they will provide a contact email or phone number in response to one of your emails about purchasing.

If they do not, you can try to provide your contact info, but be prepared for eBay to block these types of emails often. You can split up your email address or phone number on different lines in the email to avoid this. I also like to do some Google searching to see if you can find the companies website and contact info outside of eBay. Pro sellers often have their company name or other information in their eBay user name that you can use to find more info via a search engine.

Negotiating pricing

On eBay, sellers are paying between 13-20% selling fees when they sell a product on the marketplace. You want to keep this in mind when you connect with a seller who wants to sell wholesale lots to you. Your negotiating point should START at their current sale prices, less the selling fees. Ideally, you want to pay less, but if you are just opening up a new supplier relationship, I would suggest that it's more important to get the relationship started versus getting the lowest price. You can always negotiate lower prices down the road.

Connect on LinkedIn

If your emails go unanswered, there's still another way to connect with sellers. Use the Google search option mentioned above and search LinkedIn for the company name. If you do find the company listed on LinkedIn, you will often see a list of employees that you can try to connect with and test your "can I buy from you" emails with them.

Buying to show you are credible

Another great way to connect to sellers and to find out more information about their company is just to start buying their product on eBay. Think of these purchases as investments in your business. You will often get more company info, emails, and phone numbers via email and inside of the packaging of the products you purchase. It's also a great intro email topic to be able to say, "I have been purchasing your products..."

You also want to be ready to buy in quantity, even if it's a small amount. These sellers don't want to sell one or two products to you. Starting small at 10-20 pieces will get their intention, but I would always mention that your goal is to increase your purchasing as you grow your business continually.

Ask to buy their "junk"

If you continually hit roadblocks and have not connected with sellers, one trick that has worked great for me to open new supplier relationships is the "Sell me your Junk" message. This technique starts with an email or phone call with a message like this:

"Hi, there! I see you are a <product category> reseller, and your listings show that you sell high-quality products. I have customers that want to buy slightly damaged, blemished, or defective products. Do you have any of those products that you don't want to list for sale yourself that you would be interested in selling to me?"

Many companies have products like this that they have a hard time selling. If you can add value and solve this problem for them, it is a powerful way to open a relationship. Once you have established some credibility and have a strong relationship with the seller, you can start asking about buying other (not junk) products.

I can't stress enough how good this can work. Remember that everyone wants to purchase popular, perfect condition products at low prices. By changing the narrative and going after the "junk," you are lifting your voice above all the rest. Once you start buying this type of product, focus on selling just to get as much of your investment back as possible. Even if you lose money on these sales, think of it as your Tuition as you learn about sellers and make valuable connections for your business's future.

eBay is a goldmine of information that I have used for 20+ years to make sales, make connections, and create a system of ever-increasing revenue that I am excited for you to find for your own business.

THE EBAY FEEDBACK SYSTEM

There was a time, not so long ago, when the eBay feedback system was a hellish nightmare of subjective reviews that could wipe out a seller's reputation and business in minutes. I spent 3-days on an eBay panel focused on remodeling the feedback system, and since those meetings, eBay has completely changed how feedback works on the marketplace.

The feedback overhaul is excellent news for all of us.

Now, any subjective feedback does not count towards your seller rankings. That fact, coupled with new controls on how customers rate you, has made the feedback system much more reliable for both buyers and sellers.

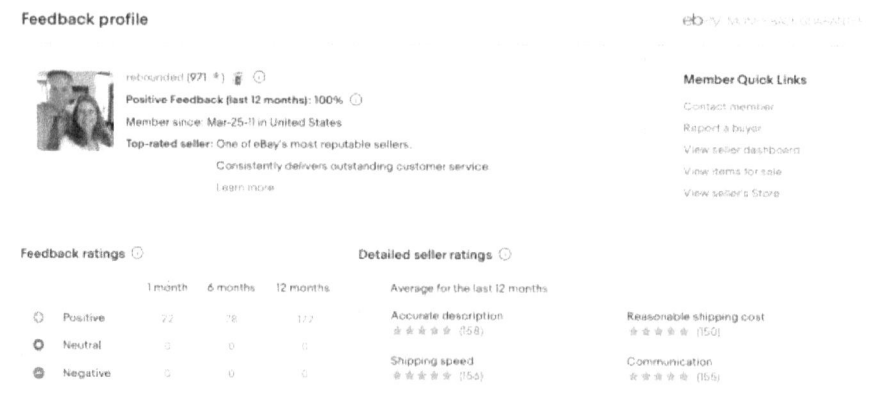

Here's how feedback works on eBay.

Feedback as a Marketing Tool

When you make a sale, you have the opportunity to leave feedback for your customer. You cannot leave negative feedback. eBay eliminated this option since many sellers left "payback" negative feedback about customers if the customer left a bad review for the seller.

You can leave comments only about your customer. I would caution you not to use the comments section to leave any negative comments or resolve customer service issues via feedback. This permanent, public feedback could be seen by potentially thousands of customers, and it is not the place to resolve customer service issues. If I have a problem customer, I just don't leave any feedback for them. Just solve the problem and move on to the next sale.

For the 99% of fantastic customers, use the feedback opportunity to send a positive message about how you communicate with customers. Remember, these public comments will be linked to the buyer's eBay account and your own eBay account. One more significant opportunity to make yourself stand out from the crowd.

Here's a snapshot of the stored feedback comments that I typically leave for customers. I get all kinds of referrals from these comments, and customers often tell me they laugh out loud when they read them. That's a good thing.

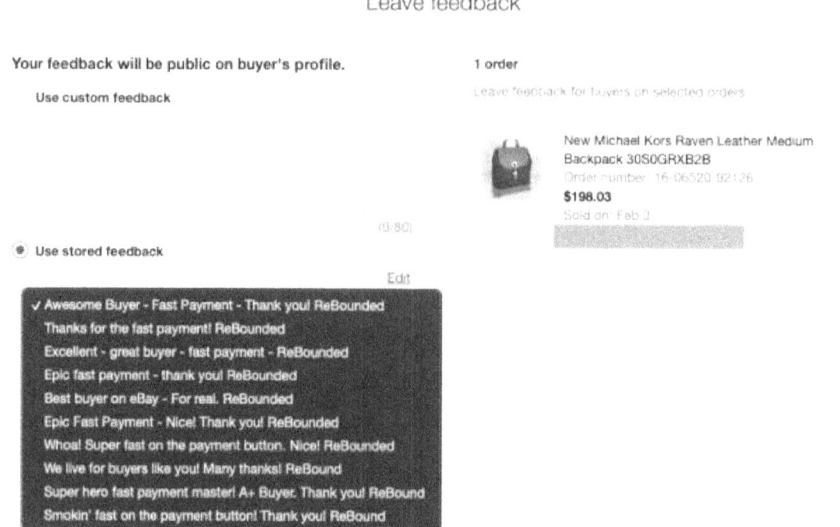

A reminder: If you are reading the print version of eBay Unlocked and you encounter blurry images, please be sure to send me a message at me@shannonjean.com, and I will send you out a crystal clear PDF version at no cost.

Using stored eBay feedback comments speeds up leaving feedback. You can make your own stored comments here: https://k2b-bulk.ebay.com/ws/eBayISAPI.dll? EditStoredComments&urlstack=5508

Automatic 5-Star Feedback

eBay will automatically give you a 5-star ranking for the following:

If you offer free shipping: automatic 5-stars for shipping charges If you ship within your designated handling time: automatic 5-stars for handling time

Buyers can rate you on your Communication only if they sent a message to you and you responded. If you did not communicate with a buyer, you will get an automatic 5-stars for the communication ranking.

Buyers can rate you on the Accurate Description of the item you are selling. So although I still believe most people don't read, you do need to have a brief, accurate description of the products you are selling. See the chapter on Your First Listing for tips on accurate descriptions.

Do you have to leave feedback for buyers?

No. You are not required to leave feedback for every sale. If you are a new eBay seller, leaving feedback is a great way to increase your engagement and visibility on the marketplace. Once you are an established seller, I suggest using the automated feedback tools in Seller Manager Pro (more on this later) or not leaving any feedback.

Getting feedback removed

Let's say you get a negative feedback from an unreasonable customer. It's bound to happen once you start making more sales. If you genuinely tried to resolve things and you feel the customer is irrational, there is a method to have negative feedback removed. This method is reserved for Top Rated Sellers. Dive into the Top-Rated Seller chapter to learn how to become one and the benefits these eBay all-stars receive.

BECOMING A TOP RATED SELLER

To be successful with any business, we need to provide excellent service to our customers on eBay or off. I'm not telling you anything you don't already know. eBay wants to reward those that provide epic service and punish or not promote those sellers who don't think it's essential to provide a high service level.

eBay has specific minimum seller standards that we all must meet to sell on their marketplace. Here's the breakdown of the different seller levels, along with why it's essential to move up the ranks to become a Top-Rated Seller as part of your system for success on eBay.

Top-Rated Seller

Let's start with the best since I know this is where you are headed. What you need to become a Top-Rated Seller:

Active eBay account for at least 90-days

100 transactions and $1000 in sales over the past 12-months

0.5% or less transaction defect percentage

0.3% or fewer cases closed by eBay without seller resolution

5% or less missed tracking uploaded on shipments

3% or less late shipments

Follow eBay Selling Practices Policy:

https://www.ebay.com/help/policies/selling-policies/selling-practices-policy?id=4346

This list may look daunting, but it's not that bad. The transaction defect percentage seems very challenging at 0.5% or less, but there are only two instances where you will get charged for a defect:

You cancel a sale because you are out of stock of an item

An item not received or item, not as described request from a buyer is closed without a response from you.

Canceling orders

To deal with the occasional order, you may need to cancel, use the technique I detail in the chapter on Cancelling Orders. This is a critical tactic. You also want to closely monitor your inventory, especially if you are selling on other marketplaces like Poshmark, Mercari, and others.

Respond to cases!

If you get a message on eBay and via email about an order not being received or an item not described, just be sure you respond to the opened case. You just need to get involved and offer a resolution to the customer.

Item not received cases

Do your research before you respond. Track the order, be sure you shipped it, and see if the carrier made a delivery attempt. Provide the tracking and additional information to the buyer. See the chapter on Customer Service for tips on messaging during these situations. You want to be friendly and courteous with the goal of getting the customer on your side, especially if you shipped the order out to them on time.

Item not as described cases

In most cases, a good return policy solves this one. If your buyer knows you offer a generous 30-day return policy, chances are they won't open an item, not as described case, instead they will just request to return the item. This is reason enough to offer 30-day returns. Most customers are not going to return your items. The ones that want to return an item are going to do it one way or another. If you don't offer returns, they will open an item, not as described case and get eBay involved. Avoid those complaints with your return policy!

5% or less missed tracking on orders

If you use eBay shipping or a third-party shipping service connected with eBay, you won't have any problem with this. As you create each order's shipping label, the tracking information will be automatically uploaded to eBay and matched up to the order.

3% or less late shipments

This is where you need to look at your handling time settings. Can you ship within 1-business day (M-F)? If you can't, then be sure to select 2-business days as your handling time. You are better off starting at 2-day handling and then work your way up if you need more time.

Benefits of being a Top Rated Seller

Higher search ranking

eBay wants buyers to have a great experience in their marketplace. When shoppers search for a product, what type of sellers do you think eBay will promote to the top of the search results? You guessed it, Top Rated Sellers. This is part of the Best Match search results that are the default setting for eBay search. If you are a TRS and another seller is not, your listings will show up higher in the search results.

Discounted selling fees

You will get a 10% discount on selling fees as a Top Rated Seller.

Additional seller protections

If you are a TRS, eBay is in your corner. They will back you up if you get false Item Not as Described claims and issue credits for return shipping labels you may have sent on a claim.

eBay allows TRS's to deduct up to 50% of any item's value if it returned in a different condition than it was sold in. This is huge. If a buyer uses a product and then returns it or does not return the complete product (missing boxes, accessories, for example), you will be able to deduct a portion of the sale price to cover the loss of value for the product.

All of this should be enough to encourage you to strive to be a Top Rated Seller. Hopefully, this just happens naturally based on your accurate product listings and epic customer service. Have more questions about TRS? Send them to me@shannonjean.com, and I will be glad to help in any way I can.

Above Standard Seller

Above Standard is where all sellers start. You are meeting the minimum standards to sell on eBay. I will not spend time on this level because there are no additional benefits to meeting the minimum requirements.

Below Standard Seller

Below Standard, as you would expect, is not a good place to be. If your transaction defect rate is above 2% or your cases closed without seller resolutions is above 0.3%.

You can learn more about Above and Below Standard seller levels on the eBay website here:
https://www.ebay.com/help/selling/seller-levels-performance-standards/seller-levels-performance-standards?id=4080

CANCELING ORDERS – WHY AND HOW

You will sometimes have to cancel an eBay order. Your customer may request to cancel before shipment; you may be out of stock of an item, there may be an error in the listing, or some other reason.

Order cancellations are not considered a positive type of engagement with eBay. In fact, order cancellations can hurt your selling status. There are a right way and a wrong way to cancel an order. Let's discuss.

When you make a sale, eBay will send you an email confirmation and alert you in the eBay App. Let's say you are checking orders, and you find out that you oversold a product and can't ship the eBay order. If you are a high-volume seller, an occasional cancellation may not hurt your seller status but is counted as a transaction defect by eBay. You want to limit these transaction defects to reach or keep your Top Rated Seller status.

Back to that order, you oversold. My suggestion is to be very proactive and accountable for the mistake and immediately reach out to the buyer. Explain the situation AND offer an alternative product if you have it. You want to phrase your message like this:

Dear <Name>,

I'm so sorry, but I oversold the product that you ordered. I am a small business owner, and I had this product listed for sale on several marketplaces. The handbag sold on another market-place, and before I could remove it from eBay, your order was placed.

Again, my sincere apologies for this mistake on my part.

I have this bag available in brown, and I would be glad to ship out the brown version. If you don't fall in love with the brown after receiving it, returns are quick, easy, and free.

Please let me know if you would like to try the brown version or prefer to cancel the order. Thank you again.

-Shannon

Of course, you know I have this statement saved via a text automation app, so I don't have to write it over and over. Be sure to see the chapter on text automation for more info.

What I am doing, in this case, is being accountable, apologizing, and offering an alternative product. Equally important, I am asking the customer to choose. Choose between the alternative or request to cancel the order.

When the customer requests to cancel, eBay does not consider it a transaction defect. This message puts the customer in the position to accept an alternative item or request to cancel.

If the customer requests to cancel the order, I always follow up with a coupon towards a future purchase:

Dear <Name>,

Thank you for the quick reply, and again, my apologies for not being able to fulfill the order. Please contact me if there is an-other handbag you are interested in so I can be sure to provide you a discounted price before purchase.

Be well,
Shannon

You will then locate the order on your shipping list and select to cancel:

On the next page, you will select Buyer Requested to Cancel from the list of options:

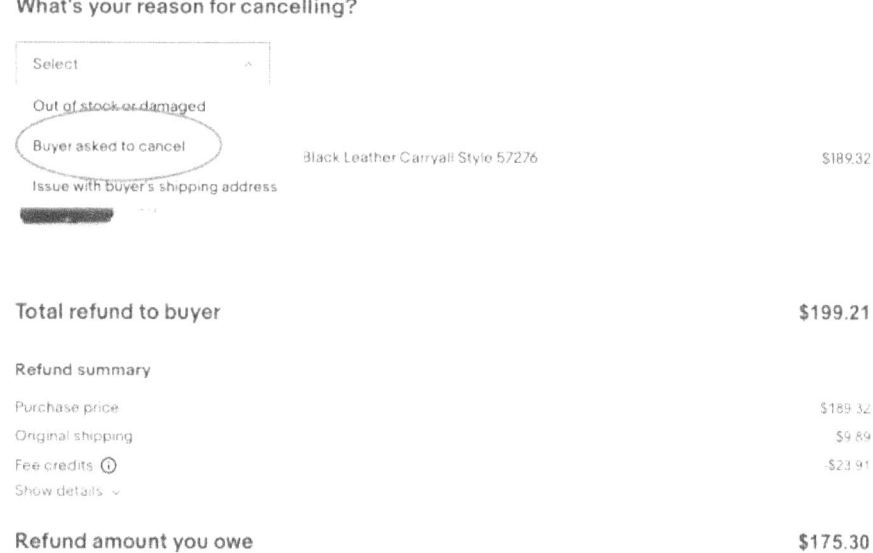

eBay may ask you if you want to relist the item for sale. Since you are out of stock, that would be a big no on that option.

We all want to keep order cancellations to a minimum, and sometimes you won't be able to use the Buyer Requested Cancellation method described here. However, I would suggest you bookmark this page since I know it will come in handy for you in the future.

WHAT TO DO WHEN YOUR SALES ARE SLOW?

If you are a marketplace seller on platforms like Poshmark, eBay, Tradesy, and others, there will be times when sales are on fire and other times when they are in the toilet. How you react during each sales phase can help create a system for success, so you spend less time in that toilet and more time shipping orders.

Selling on multiple marketplaces

When you have product listings spread across various channels, you can quickly see if the entire market has slowed down or if there is a problem with a particular marketplace or product line you are offering. I currently sell on three marketplaces + wholesale.

I've been selling on eBay for 18+ years, primarily in the technology and electronics categories, then moving into the fashion categories over the past 3-4 years. Even though the products and customers are entirely different, the sales tactics and best practices are the same.

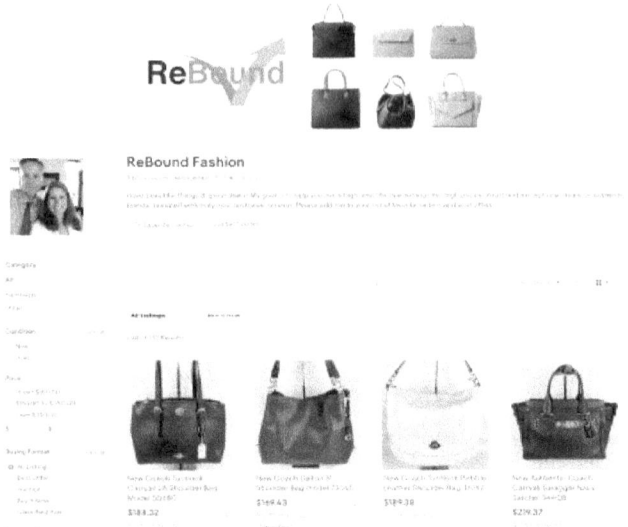

I joined Poshmark to start an experiment to see if I could create a business solely using my phone. I started with zero followers and zero sales, eventually building my sales to over $750,000 with over 250,000 followers. I found my niche in the handbag market, and in 2019 I wrote Poshmark Unlocked to share my experience and help other sellers on their path to success.

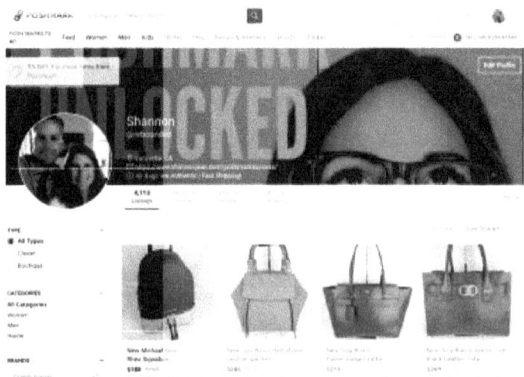

Tradesy is the third marketplace that I have found success. A completely different animal than eBay and Poshmark, but valuable for a specific demographic that, in my experience, is willing to pay more for higher-end designer brands.

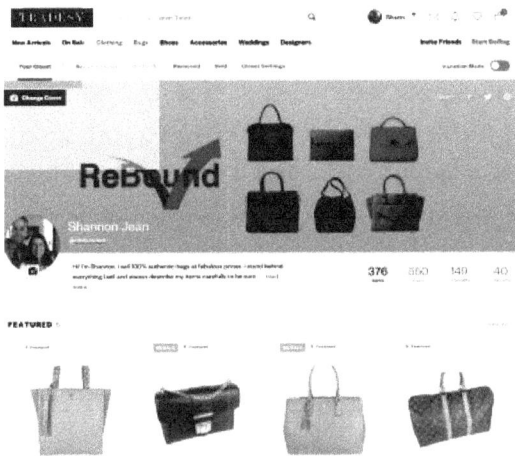

What to do when things stop selling?

First – Check your data!

What time of year is it?

Are you in the usual summer slowdown? After holiday buying burnout? Do you have previous years' sales data to check against the current period? Looking at my historical data always helps to keep me from flipping out when things get slow. With a quick check of my sales database, I can see what things looked like last year and if the sales slowdown is seasonal.

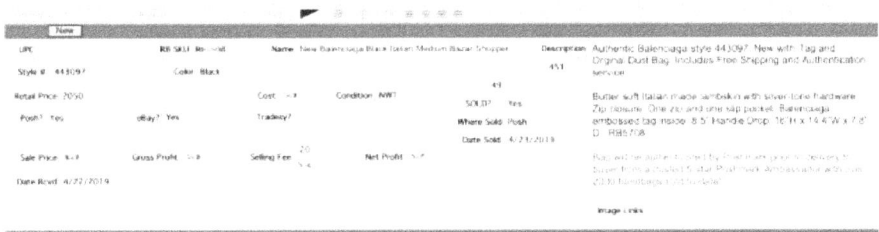

What brands are you selling?

If you are a reseller, check to see if your brand mix has changed and if that could be impacting your sales. Also, check sizes for clothing since the market for Small may not be great, and your XL inventory could be sold out.

Keeping a historical database of sales is critically important for you to recognize seasonal sales shifts, brand sales, product sizing, and much more. I use Filemaker Pro to track my sales data. You can use any database application like AirTable or an accounting package like QuickBooks to track sales and inventory data.

Once you have an idea of what is going on, use your time wisely.

If you're in the middle of a seasonal slowdown, spend time to improve your business and be ready for when sales pick back up:
Get more followers on social channels and marketplaces like Poshmark
Work on your photography skills with an online class or new lighting
Grow your social presence on Instagram, Facebook, and Pinterest
Focus on connecting with new suppliers.
Research your niche. Are you still competitively priced?
Connect with other sellers to see if their business has slowed as well

Overall, don't panic. Use your time wisely to improve your business and your connections. Slowdowns happen to everyone, and many times they are caused by outside factors beyond our control. By researching your internal processes, you can be sure to correct any problems that are within your control.

BULK EDITING YOUR EBAY LISTINGS

There are countless third-party applications and services to help you manage your eBay listings in bulk. Since I am focused on eBay services, let's jump in and talk about how to bulk edit your listings with eBay's built-in tools.

Start by heading over to your Active Listings. If you have made at least one sale on eBay, you will be using Seller Hub and hover your mouse pointer over the Listings tab and select Active Listings. No sales yet? Just click My eBay link in the upper right of any eBay page > Selling.

Once you have your list of Active Listings up, select which listings you want to edit, or click the checkbox above the listings to select all listings shown on the page.

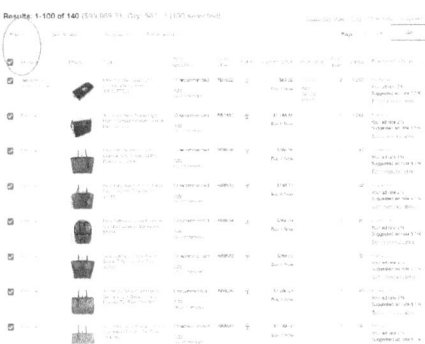

You can then choose to Edit the selected listings or Edit all of your listings from the Edit menu. The next view will be of your chosen listings in the bulk edit tool.

You can customize which fields you want to edit by clicking the Customize link. For this example, I have limited the fields to keep the image snapshot smaller. Add or remove whichever fields you want on this screen.

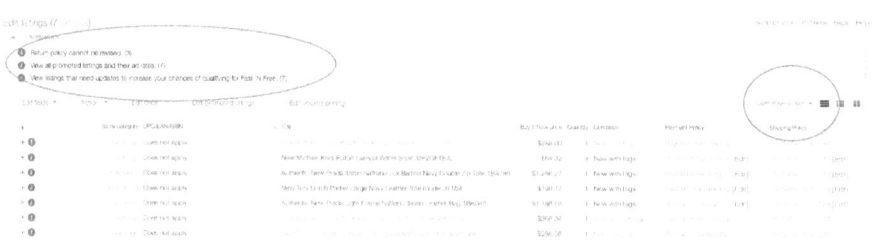

You will also see some messages about the listings. eBay is showing a red ! for listings that cannot be modified. In my case, those red alert listings have Offers to Watchers that I sent out earlier in the day. Those offers are active for 24-hours, so those listings cannot be modified. eBay will also give you tips for making changes if you want to qualify for specific programs like fast and free shipping promotions.

Two ways to Bulk Edit

Some fields like Price and Quantity are editable by just clicking into the fields. You can also use this method to edit right from the Active Listing screen. The real productivity enhancer is the second method.

Select which listings to edit again, then click the Edit Fields link to select which fields you want to Bulk Edit. Fields like shipping options, return policies, and more are listed.

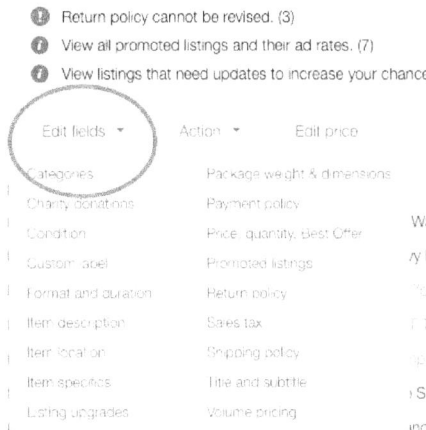

Make your selection, and then make your edits. That's it! Just click the Save Listings button at the bottom of the screen when you are finished bulk editing.

INVENTORY
TRACKING

I mentioned tracking your sales in the previous chapter, but I want to take some more time to focus on the importance of monitoring your inventory daily.

If you already own a business and have been selling products for some time, the chances are good that you already have an inventory tracking and reporting system in place. If you do, I believe you can adapt your current system to work with your eBay store.

If you are not yet tracking and managing your inventory, this section is for you. **Keeping track of your products is a critical part of success with your business – both on and off eBay.**

You need to track your product inventory so you can access the following info:

- Quantity of product in stock
  Cost of products
- Product condition
- Product details, description, model, style, etc
- Sale prices

- Net Profit per product (Sale Price – Fees – Cost of Goods Sold)
- Sales trends
- more

Experiment and find a system that works best for you. Here's the workflow that I find to be very quick and easy. I usually sell unique items, meaning I am not buying hundreds of one thing and selling it repeatedly. For large quantity sales of the same item, you would want to adjust as needed to increase efficiency.

I create a unique SKU (product ID) for each item I sell. If I am selling the same things in quantity, I simply add a -1, -2 when I sell the item for my sales record.

I use Filemaker Pro to track all of my Poshmark sales. I created a database with fields specific to my product line (handbags). Every-single-item I sell gets a record. **I can use this to track item costs, how long I've had the item, when it sells, gross profit, selling fees, net profit, product title, and description.** When I get more of the same thing in stock, I just duplicate the record and change the SKU. This is a huge timesaver!

Would you like an empty version of this database for your use? Simply send an email to me@shannonjean.com, and I will hook you up. You will need to purchase FileMaker Pro to use this database. There are plenty of lower-cost databases available, and you can use some free solutions like Libre Base, Airtable, and more.

If you don't want to or are not comfortable setting up your database, you can also use an accounting program like Quickbooks to track your inventory and manage your accounting. The critical takeaway is to do something – you have to keep accurate records and know the status of your inventory at all times if you are going to make real money selling on eBay.

WHY RANDOM PRICING IS SO POWERFUL

Years ago, my accountant for one of our businesses told me we would have increased our profits by about $10K if we had just added $0.99 to every item we sold in the past year. Even though I was not a big fan of the $0.99 ending on every price, I couldn't ignore the missed profits.

Poshmark only allows you to enter a dollar amount for your sale price with no options for cents. On eBay and Tradesy, you can list an exact price, so I have always added the $0.99 suffix to each product. Earlier this year, I decided to experiment with those cents to see if I could change buyers' behavior.

Here's what I did:

Instead of merely ending each product listing with a $0.99 or $0.98 (as in $49.98 or $198.99), I started to put odd prices on products to try to catch the eye of a potential customer that was scrolling through search results.

I began to use random suffixes like $0.13, $0.71, $0.82, and so on. I wanted to see if those weird prices would attract a buyer's attention. Sounds crazy, I know. So instead of $49.98, I would use $49.61, and $198.99 became $198.76.

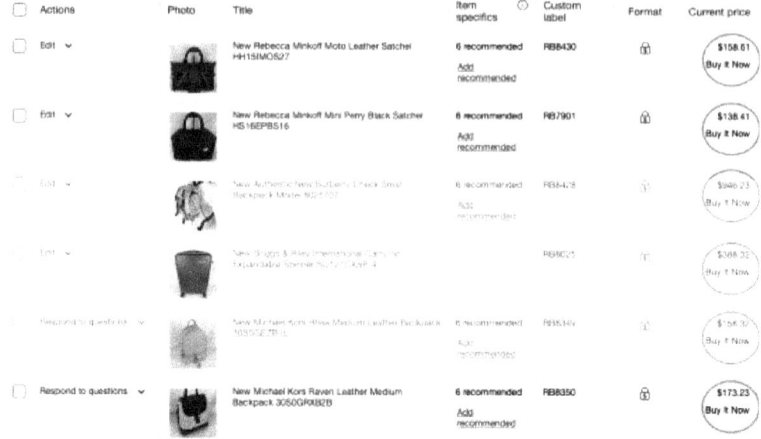

When I began this experiment on certain products; I saw an immediate increase in sales. Not a huge amount, but handbags that were slow movers started selling with an increase of 11%. With that result, I changed the rest of my 175+ eBay and Tradesy listings to this new pricing structure, and I have seen an increase in both listing views and sales. Overall I continue to see just about an 8% increase in sales.

Moral of the story: Every Dollar Counts!

Bonus moral: Keep trying new things. I have been selling for 20+ years and have never tried this before since I didn't "like how the price looked" with a funny amount at the end. Who knew!?

OFFERS TO WATCHERS

When potential buyers are browsing your product listings and want to keep a list of items they are interested in, they add the product listing to their Watch List.

Once a product is added to a potential buyers list, you will be alerted and allowed to send a discounted offer to all "watchers." eBay refers to this feature as Offers to Watchers. Here's how it works and how I suggest you use it.

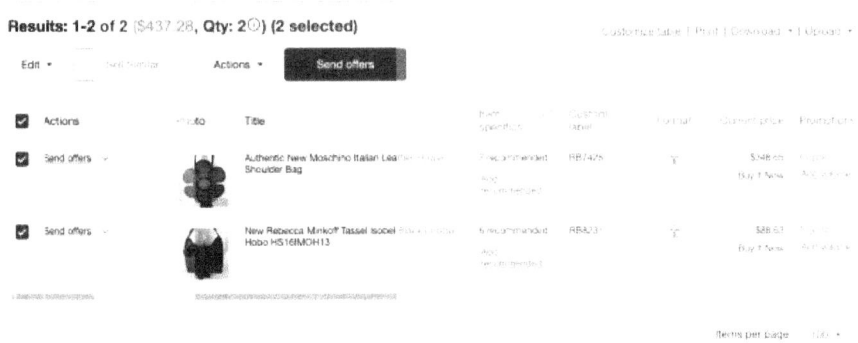

When you view a list of your active listings, you will see a Send Offer link when someone has added that product to their watch list. Before you make your first sale, you will have to send out offers individually for each product. If multiple people have added the product to their Watch List, you can send the request out to them simultaneously. Once you make your first eBay sale and are using Seller Hub, you will be able to send out offers on multiple product listings simultaneously. Let's walk through both methods:

Individual Offer to Watchers

Click the Send Offer link next to any of your product listings. If there is no Send Offer option, it means no one has added the product to a Watch List.

Enter a dollar amount or a percentage off the product price that you would like to offer. Stop – let's talk about messaging before you click the Send Offer button.

Offer Messaging

With each offer you send out, you have an opportunity to communicate with potential buyers. This is a great time to stand out with a few quick sentences to encourage the potential buyer to act fast to get the deal. Here's the message I have found to be most effective:

Hi!

I see that you are watching this handbag. Here's a discount offer that may help.

Please note that this offer is being sent to multiple potential buyers, so the bag is subject to being sold at any time.

Cheers!
Shannon

--

Why this message works

The power of the exclamation point! It's tough to show excitement in a quick email that most people won't read. I always start with an excited Hi! to get their attention.

I then point out that I noticed that they added the product to their Watch List followed up with my "offer to help." I am trying to build trust and credibility here.

I want to encourage the potential buyer to act fast and to know they could lose this deal. My last sentence informs them that I am sending this offer out to more than just one person and that it's first-come, first-served, and the product may be sold if they don't act fast.

Finally, I end with more excitement, using Cheers! with my name to make the message more personal.

I see excellent conversions with this message. I suggest you work with a few different messages to find what works best for you. Test, measure, and then make a data-driven decision.

Enter your message and then click the Send Offer to Buyer button. Now you wait. One key element to understand about Offers to Watchers is that eBay does not require immediate payment from the buyer when they accept your offer at the time of this writing. Crazy, I know. This can be frustrating if you are selling unique items (like my handbag business) because the product cannot be purchased by anyone else while waiting for the buyer to make payment. eBay gives the buyer up to 48-hours to make the payment.

If you are selling quantities of the same product over and over, waiting for payment may not be an issue for you. For unique item sellers, I use a trick to encourage fast payments when you have time to contact the buyer. I send a message like this when a buyer has accepted an offer but has not made payment.
--
Hi!

Thanks for your order! I am glad I was able to offer you a discount on this item.

Please make the payment for the order as quickly as you can. Since I only have one of these handbags and I have the bag listed for sale on multiple marketplaces, the bag is subject to being sold at any time before final payment is made.

Thank you again! I will confirm when I receive your payment.

Cheers!
Shannon
--

I want the buyer to know that if they don't make the payment quickly, the bag could be sold on another marketplace. If that happens, I will cancel the order on eBay.

Before you do cancel, consider the negative engagement impact to your account on eBay. Since I am making significant sales each month on my account, canceling an occasional order is not that big of a deal. If you are a new seller or only selling a small volume each month, I would not recommend canceling any orders unless you use the buyer requested to cancel method I describe in eBay Unlocked.

Sending Offers to Watchers for multiple product listings

Once you begin to use Seller Hub (after your first sale), you will have the option to send out multiple discount offers at one time. This is how I typically start my day on eBay – reviewing how many products were added to potential buyers' Watch List within the last 24-hours and sending out offers on those products.

I use the same message as I describe above when sending out multiple Offers to Watchers, and I make sales just about every-single-day using this method.

How much to discount?

Great question. The answer depends on what products you are selling and how much Return on Investment (ROI) you are looking for with each sale. Since I am selling higher-priced items ($300-$2500), my discount is typically around 5%. If I was selling $50 items, maybe 10% is more appropriate.

You should experiment and, you guessed it, test and measure to find out what works for you. I keep hammering you to make data-driven decisions because those are decisions that have an impact. Your gut instinct may tell you to go one way, but if the data doesn't back it up, you know what to do.

ENGAGEMENT – WHAT IT IS AND WHY IT'S SO IMPORTANT

What's an algorithm? The official definition looks like this:

"a process or set of rules to be followed in calculations or other problem-solving operations, especially by a computer."

For our purposes, let's consider the eBay algorithm as a set of rules and instructions that eBay programs into their marketplace to make decisions. Lots of decisions. Decisions about which product listing to put at the top of the search results list, about what sellers to recommend to buyers, what products to recommend, and thousands more.

Your job is to build your eBay business, create your product listings, handle shipments, and manage your customer service to take advantage of these decisions to become highly recommended by the eBay algorithm.

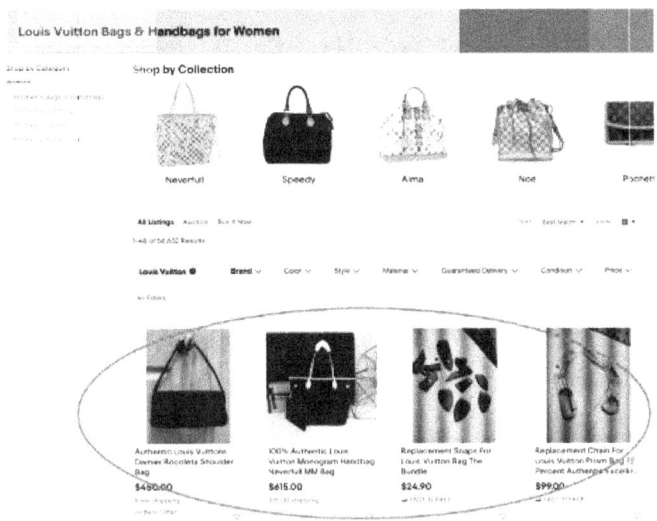

In this section, I will be focusing on engagement and how to increase it to build your success on eBay. Listings shown in the top row of the image above are there for a reason: eBay is promoting these sellers based on their performance and positive engagement with the marketplace.

When I use the word engagement, I am referring to your interactions with the eBay marketplace. Engagement includes creating listings, modifying listings, sending out offers to buyers, answering questions from the message center, shipping orders, and more.

eBay is monitoring the frequency and type of engagement you have with their marketplace. The more positive engagement they see, the more they will promote your listings, refer buyers to you, offer you discounts, and consider you a credible seller working in buyers' best interests.

Positive types of engagement

New Listings: If you can create new listings every day on eBay, you will be more successful. I know this may be hard, but there are ways to automate this and streamline listing creation that we will discuss more.

Editing Listings: if you are updating your listings daily, you will see more success. Editing things like pricing, quantity available, and more will show eBay that you are actively managing your listings

Replying to messages – quickly: eBay is tracking how long it takes to reply to messages. The quicker you respond, the better the engagement. I suggest you use the eBay app on your phone to get alerts and react quickly to questions. You will also make more sales when you answer potential buyers' questions quickly.

Sending offers to Watchers: when interested buyers add your product to their Watch List, you will have the option to send them a discounted offer. You can do this for single listings or in bulk on many product listings at once. I will spend more time with you showing you how this will help you increase your sales.

Giving feedback: you can only leave positive feedback for buyers. You should leave feedback when you can, especially when just getting started. It not only increases your positive engagement but it helps to build your credibility with other potential buyers.

Ship fast and provide tracking: When you ship within your stated shipping timeframe (set by you in the Business Policies section), eBay rewards you with positive engagement. The same happens when you provide accurate tracking numbers for each shipment.

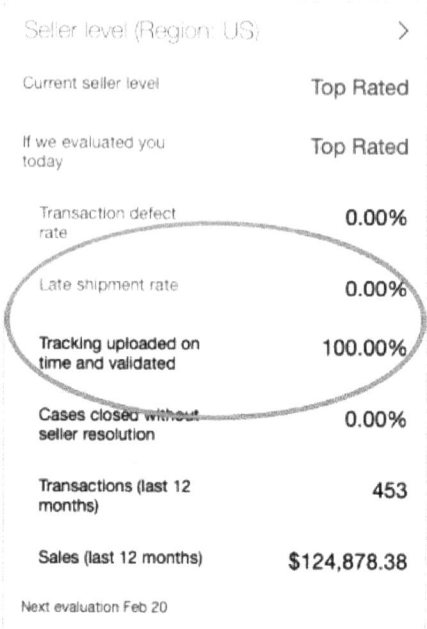

Seller level (Region: US)	>
Current seller level	Top Rated
If we evaluated you today	Top Rated
Transaction defect rate	0.00%
Late shipment rate	0.00%
Tracking uploaded on time and validated	100.00%
Cases closed without seller resolution	0.00%
Transactions (last 12 months)	453
Sales (last 12 months)	$124,878.38

Next evaluation Feb 20

Along with being rewarded for positive engagement, you can be penalized for the wrong type of engagement.

Negative types of engagement

Having buyer complaints filed against your account

Receiving negative feedback

Not responding to complaints (cases) filed by a buyer

Canceling orders (use the buyer requested method to offset)

Not leaving feedback for your buyers

Not shipping orders within your stated shipping timeframe

Not providing tracking information for your shipments

By focusing on increasing your positive engagement and limiting your negative engagement, you will have eBay on your side as you build your eBay business.

PROMOTED LISTINGS

Want to get your listings pushed to the top of searched results quickly? Let's talk about Promoted Listings.

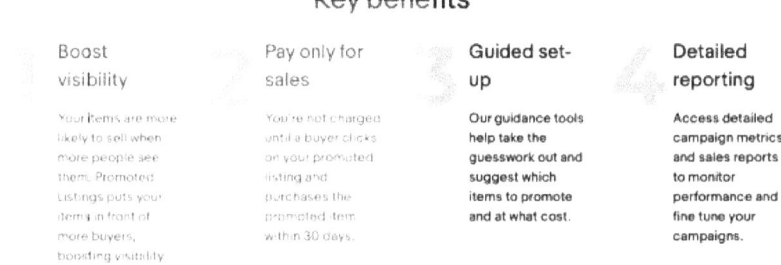

eBay's description of what Promoted Listings can do for you as a seller:

Promoted Listings helps your items stand out among billions of listings on eBay and be seen by millions of active buyers when they're browsing and searching for what you are selling, helping to increase the likelihood of a sale. The best part? You only pay when your item sells.

Promoted Listings are available to Above Standard and Top Rated sellers with recent sales activity.

https://pages.ebay.com/seller-center/listing-and-marketing/promoted-listings.html

Promoted Listings allow you to pay an additional percentage to eBay to get your product listings shown in front of more potential buyers. eBay suggests that you can see an increase in sales of up to 36% by using Promoted Listings.

You can choose to promote a product when you create a new listing or after. I typically wait a few days after I list a new product since it may sell on its own without paying the additional fees.

eBay will kindly suggest a percentage rate to use when you want to promote a listing. This percentage is based on what other sellers have used in the category you are selling in. I suggest you ignore this suggestion and use the data-driven decisions process to test out the smallest percentage first, then increase it if needed.

I typically use 2% as a quick and easy rule for promoting my listings. This small amount still keeps my overall eBay selling fees to about 12% while it puts my listings in front of thousands of additional buyers. As of this writing, 47% of my sales come through Promoted Listings.

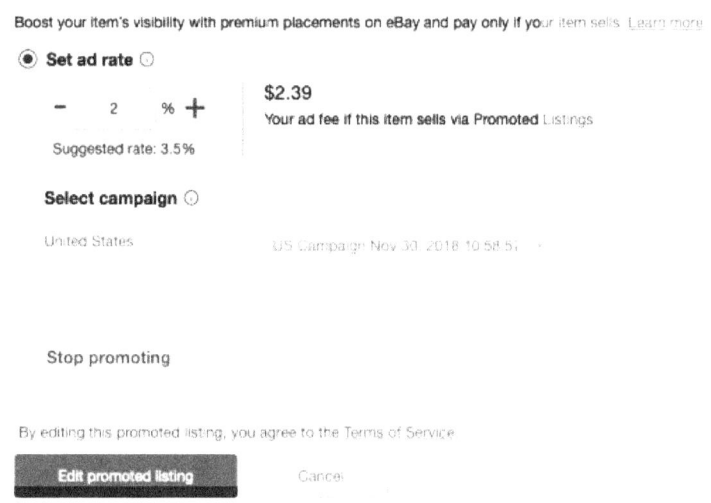

Promoted Listings are a powerful method to increase your sales quickly. I suggest using it by testing on various listings to see which type of products benefit from using it. Test and measure the results!

THE INTERESTING WORLD OF EBAY FEES

You know that I love eBay, but I will admit that their fee structure can be a bit wonky and sometimes challenging to figure out. The good news is that the fees are getting more straightforward, and there is a quick way to find out what your average eBay fees are currently, even if that number can change frequently.

Let's start at the start. A bunch of stuff impacts eBay fees. Things like:

Managed Payments Y/N
Selling Category
Type of listing: Fixed Price or Auction
Account standing: Top Rated Seller?
Listing upgrades
Promoted listing?
Store Subscription
eBay promotions

As I write this, eBay is in the middle of a massive shift away from outside payment processors like PayPal to its own managed payment platform. Since this is the future of payments on eBay, this chapter will focus on the Managed Payments fee structure. If you would like to see the classic Selling Fees that are on their way out, here's the link:
https://www.ebay.com/help/selling/fees-credits-invoices/selling-fees?id=4364

eBay charges two main types of fees: an Insertion Fee when you create a product listing and a Final Value Fee if your item sells.

Insertion fees are typically $0.35 per listing. There are specific high dollar product categories like Heavy Equipment, Commercial Printing Presses (who knew!?), and Food Trucks, Trailers, and Carts that have a $20 Insertion Fee. eBay also runs promotions all the time, with some categories have zero insertion fees. As I type this, Athletic Shoes over $100 have a $0 insertion fee, as do Guitars and Bases. There are also some other categories with higher Insertion Fees such as Real Estate,

You can avoid some listing fees. The easiest way is to subscribe to an eBay Store to receive 200 listings per month with $0 listing fees. eBay also runs promotions that can sometimes offer up to 500 listings. You will find these promos in your email and the Seller Hub section.

When you list your products, you can choose from all kinds of upgrades that will add to the cost of selling your products on eBay. Here's a sample:

Good 'Til Cancelled listings*

Optional listing upgrade	Item price of $150 or less	Item price of more than $150	Classified Ad format or Real Estate listings
Bold	$4.00	$6.00	$4.00
Gallery Plus Free for listings in the Collectibles, Art, Pottery & Glass, and Antiques categories	$1.00	$2.00	$1.00
List in two categories	Insertion and optional listing upgrade fees apply for each category. The higher of the two final value fees is charged, if your item sells		
Listing Designer	$0.30	$0.60	$0.30
Scheduled Listing	Free	Free	$0.10 (free for Real Estate listings)
Subtitle	$1.50	$6.00	$1.50

Do these upgrades help sell your products faster and increase your profits? That's a great question, and only you can answer it. The key is to experiment and track the results. You might try using the Bold upgrade on one listing and no Bold on the next to see which one sells faster. Adding another category may help you sell more, maybe not. Is a subtitle what you need to be successful? Could be. I don't use these upgrades, but I always defer to the "test and see for yourself" method since I don't know what you will be selling.

When you make a sale, eBay charges you a Final Value Fee. And guess what? This amount also varies and depends on a bunch of different things. Here's a quick rundown on Final Value Fees (as of January 2021).

eBay currently charges 12.35% + $0.30 per order on the total amount of the sale for MOST categories. The total amount includes shipping charges if you charge for shipping since eBay is continuously trying to seduce you into offering free shipping by pointing out various savings and promotional programs. If you sell high-dollar products, this fee drops to 2.35% on the portion of the sale over $7500.

Final Value fees vary based on the categories you sell in and your products' total sale price. Here's a snapshot:

Category	Insertion fee	Final value fee % + $0.30 per order
Most categories, including Music > Records, eBay Motors > Parts & Accessories, and eBay Motors > Automotive Tools & Supplies. For vehicles, see our Motors fees.		• 12.35% on total amount of the sale up to $7,500 calculated per item • 2.35% on the portion of the sale over $7,500
Books DVDs & Movies Music (except **Records** category)	First 200 listings free per month, then $0.35 per listing	• 14.35% on total amount of the sale up to $7,500 calculated per item • 2.35% on the portion of the sale over $7,500
Jewelry & Watches > Watches, Parts & Accessories > **Watches**		• 12.35% on total amount of the sale up to $1,000 calculated per item • 6.5% on the portion of the sale over $1,000 up to $7,500 calculated per item • 2.35% on the portion of the sale over $7,500
Select Business & Industrial categories: • Heavy Equipment Parts & Attachments > **Heavy Equipment** • Printing & Graphic Arts > **Commercial Printing Presses** • Restaurant & Food Service > **Food Trucks, Trailers & Carts**	$20	• 4.35% on total amount of the sale up to $15,000 calculated per item • 2.35% on the portion of the sale over $15,000
Musical Instruments & Gear > **Guitars & Basses**	Free	• 5.85% on total amount of the sale up to $7,500 calculated per item • 2.35% on the portion of the sale over $7,500
Select Clothing, Shoes & Accessories categories: • Men > Men's Shoes > **Athletic Shoes**	Free if starting price is $100 or	• 0% if total amount of the sale is $100 or more. The $0.30 per order fee will be credited back

How to save on Final Value Fees

You can save on your Final Value Fees by becoming a Top Rated Seller on eBay. You can read the specific details about Top Rated Seller status in the chapter on Performance Standards. Here it's important to know that eBay discounts your fees by 10% if you maintain your Top Rated Seller status. There are many more benefits of TRS status that you should read about in the Performance Standards chapter.

How to pay higher Final Value Fees

If you slip below eBay's minimum performance standards, you can expect an increase of 5% to your Final Value Fees for the next 30-days as you try to climb out of the gutter. You slip below the minimum standards by doing things like shipping later than your stated handling time, not responding to customer complaints promptly, and more. Since you are the type of business owner that purchased this book, I know you won't have a problem with these standards. Read the Performance Standards chapter for more of the gruesome details.

Promoted Listings

If you use the Promoted Listings feature, you will also need to add that percentage to your Final Value Fees. In the example I used in the Promoted Listings chapter, you would add 2% to the Final Value Fee of any product sold via Promoted Listings.

Dispute Fee

If a customer files a credit card dispute related to an item you sold them, you may be charged a $20 Dispute Fee. Good customer service will generally avoid this.

International Fee

Suppose you sell internationally direct to customers or use the eBay Global Shipping Program. In that case, you will be assessed an additional fee if your product is sold to an international buyer or you ship outside the US. This fee is currently 1.65% of the total amount of your sale.

Getting a Dashboard View of Fees

There is a central location to see what your overall eBay fees are at any time or for a given period. Find this in the Seller Hub, under the Performance tab. My fees added up to 17% from December 26, 2020 – January 25, 2021.

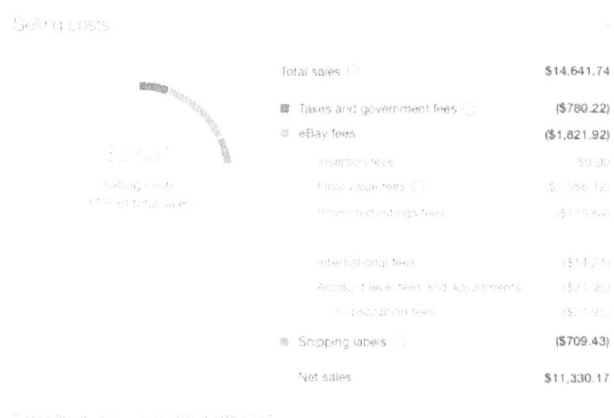

Are eBay fees too high?

That depends. Finding customers always costs money. There are always fees and costs associated with making sales. Can you reach millions of customers with fees that cost less than eBay? Maybe. Only you know what it costs to make a sale.

Many marketplaces charge 20% or more in fees. I believe eBay's fee structure is pretty balanced for the services and exposure they offer. What do you think? Remember you can always connect with me via email at me@shannonjean.com or via the private Unlocked Group here: https://www.facebook.com/groups/poshmarkunlocked

SELLING ON MULTIPLE MARKETPLACES

This book is all about selling on eBay, but I believe strongly that a long-term system for success should include selling on other marketplaces. Why? Simply put, different people like to shop differently. Some buyers trust eBay and are comfortable shopping there, while some younger buyers may love Poshmark or Mercari and stick with them. Higher-end buyers may like The RealReal or Tradesy.

Why not expose your business to each of these markets?

I think much of the decision about which marketplaces to sell on is all about time: your time. What is the best use of your time with regards to:

• How long does it take to list products for sale on the marketplace?

• What is your Average Sale Price on each marketplace? Net Profits?

• Are the customers more demanding on a particular marketplace? How much time are you spending on customer service issues? I hear many Mercari horror stories that have kept me off the platform with high-end handbags.

• What sort of Pro/Business seller support is there? You are here to grow your business. The marketplace should be helping you, NOT slowing you down.

• Fees: are you paying more for less? My eBay fees (with Top Rated Seller discounts) are currently 15% vs. 20% for Poshmark. However, Poshmark's Authentication and inspection service for handbags over $500 are well worth the extra fees.

• Connections: I keep harping on this, but can you connect with employees and executives from a marketplace? You WILL need their help someday, and if they are not open to networking on LinkedIn with you, that's a bad sign.

• Community: Is there a supportive, uplifting community of sellers that will help you succeed on the marketplace? I would say eBay and Poshmark both have done great work building their support communities. Mercari and Tradesy....meh.

If you are just getting started with marketplace selling, I would suggest mastering one marketplace first, then expanding. Learn as much as you need to succeed with eBay, for example, before moving on to Poshmark. You will need time to fine-tune your business, your customer service, shipping, and more. Once you have had some success and worked out the kinks on the systems you need to make your business work; it's time to start cross-listing on other marketplaces.

Poshmark Unlocked

Poshmark is one such marketplace that I have found success on selling handbags, licensed NFL gear, shoes, and more.

Poshmark Unlocked shares my journey from zero followers, zero sales, and zero knowledge about the fashion business to over $750K in sales and 250,000 followers. With over 250 pages of content, you will learn everything you need to know about building a successful business on the Poshmark Social Commerce marketplace.

And just like eBay Unlocked, Poshmark Unlocked includes my Love it, or it's Free Guarantee. If you don't find the book helpful in building your business on Poshmark, just contact me for a full refund.

Find Poshmark Unlocked here:

https://shannonjean.com/books

AVOID THE FREE SHIPPING TRAP

A bit more about so-called free shipping: it's worth experimenting with, but also worth pointing out that you do not have to offer free shipping to sell on eBay successfully.

You will read countless articles and hear recommendations over and over about why you should offer free shipping. I disagree with this general statement and suggest that many factors should impact your decision to offer free shipping.

Here's my take on the free shipping concept: it sounds great, you offer free shipping, and you make more sales. eBay promotes your listings in search results if you offer free shipping. Buyers love free shipping.

Yes, you may make more sales. But I would argue that you should be looking more at your Net Profits than your overall sales numbers. If you are selling inexpensive items, offering free shipping can wipe out any profits. If your returns rate is high, you will eat that shipping cost when you issue a refund.

My advice is always to make data-driven decisions. Test and measure the results. Create similar listings, once with a shipping charge and another with free shipping. See how they sell, monitor returns, and then check your Net Profit. Are you making more Net Profit because more customers are buying the product with free shipping? Awesome – go ahead and use that method.

I have stopped offering free shipping for my eBay business since my testing showed that it did not significantly impact my sales. Instead, I charge a flat-rate of $9.98 for handbags. When I get returns, I don't refund that initial shipping charge unless I made an error, and the return is due to that.

Many modern marketplaces like Poshmark, Tradesy, and Mercari have stepped away from the free shipping trap. I have high praise for these companies and their realization that shipping is never "free" and that customers are OK with being charged a reasonable shipping charge.

What about Free Returns?

Free returns may sound scary, but they can pay off in multiple ways. When you offer free returns (meaning you will provide a pre-paid label for a return), it builds a tremendous amount of trust and credibility with potential customers. After offering free returns for over a year now, I can tell you that it has NOT increased the number of returns I get, which hovers between 1-2% of sales. It has increased the number of repeat customers that buy from me, and it has improved my sales by 21% on eBay.

Free returns also help when you have an upset customer that claims an item is not as described. Rather than getting into an argument about return shipping costs (because they will bring it up), just cover the cost and move on to making more sales.

Again, use the concept of the data-driven decision and test some of your listings with free returns to see how it impacts your sales. Test, measure, and make changes accordingly.

USING SOCIAL MEDIA TO PROMOTE YOUR EBAY LISTINGS

Once you have things up and running on eBay, your seller standards are hitting all the right numbers, and you are ready to expand your marketing, it's time to start promoting via social media.

I will focus social media promotion on three platforms that I think work the best for sales: Instagram, Pinterest, and Facebook. I believe that Instagram and Pinterest drive more sales while Facebook allows you to add credibility to your business and build a following over time. I have experimented and tracked the data over time and have found that Pinterest and Instagram are the most effective at attracting buyers and delivering sales for my particular businesses on eBay.

Let's start with a discussion about the often ignored power of Pinterest!

You'll be amazed at the amount of traffic that Pinterest can drive to your eBay store. You'll see thousands of referrals from this source as you increase your listings and share from eBay.

Why Pinterest?

Let's start with "Why" you should be promoting your products and services on Pinterest:

- 72% of Pinterest users report that they are inspired to shop and buy by browsing on Pinterest.
- 70% of those users say they find new products and services while browsing.
- Proportionally, Pinterest drives more buying decisions than social media platforms. 33% more than Facebook, 71% more than Snapchat, and 200% more than Twitter.

More powerful Pinterest data about selling via their platform:

- 98% of Pinterest users say they are willing to try new products or services they discover on the platform.
- 40% of Pinterest users have incomes over $100k per year.
- Check out the infographic below, and you'll see that Pinterest users are more likely to spend and spend more on products and services they find on Pinterest.

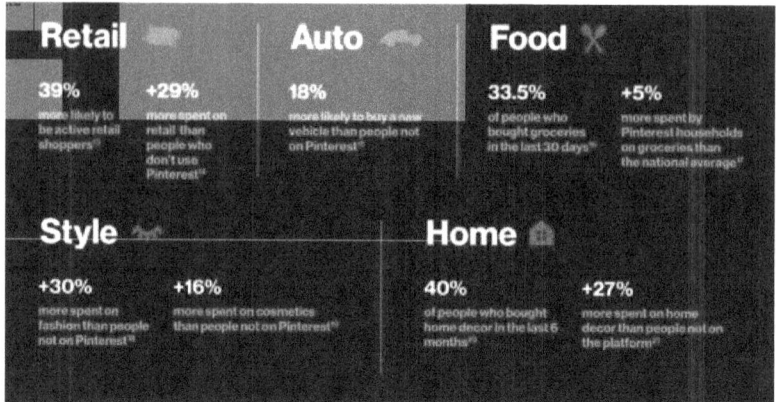

Now that you agree that there are some valuable potential customers on Pinterest, let's roll into how to set up your business account.

- Create your Pinterest Business Account. Start things off right by creating a Pinterest Business Account vs. a personal account.

https://help.pinterest.com/en/business/article/get-a-business-account

- Create your first "Boards" – you'll want to create Pinterest Boards – the places where you will "Pin" your content. We recommend being very specific with each different Board you make – stick to unique niches (The Riches are in the Niches!) for each Board. Use different Boards for additional products or different demographics you are trying to attract.

- Use keywords and hashtags for your Pins. When posting your content to your new Boards, be sure to use keywords and hashtags with each post. Pinterest offers a powerful Keyword Suggestion feature on its Promoted Pins advertising platform. You can use this to find the most popular keywords related to your product or service.

- For more additional methods of promoting your

products on Pinterest, check out this article from the eCommerce experts at Shopify: https://www.shopify.com/blog/pinterest-marketing

You can learn more about the Pinterest "Path to Purchase" here: https://business.pinterest.com/sub/business/business-infographic-download/pinterest-path-to-purchase.pdf

At the end of this chapter, I will show you the methods you can use to quickly share your eBay listings to Pinterest, Instagram, and other social channels.

Instagram Strategies to Grow Your eBay Sales

When you link your eBay Store to Instagram, you expand your store's reach and engagement with a broad audience that can be turned into customers. Here are some tips to help increase your eBay sales with Instagram.

Create an Instagram account specifically for your eBay Store

By having a separate account linked to your Posh store, you can focus your marketing efforts without mixing things up with your personal Instagram page. We suggest using your eBay Store name as your Instagram name.

Link Back to eBay

Be sure to link back to your eBay Store in your Instagram Bio – when you set up your account, you'll have a chance to enter just one website link – using the eBay website, copy the link for your store and use that URL in your Instagram bio. If you don't have an eBay Store yet, you can link to all your listings' search pages.

To create a link just to your listings, if you don't have an eBay Store, from the eBay home page, click the "Advanced" link next to the search bar. Click By Seller and enter your seller name.

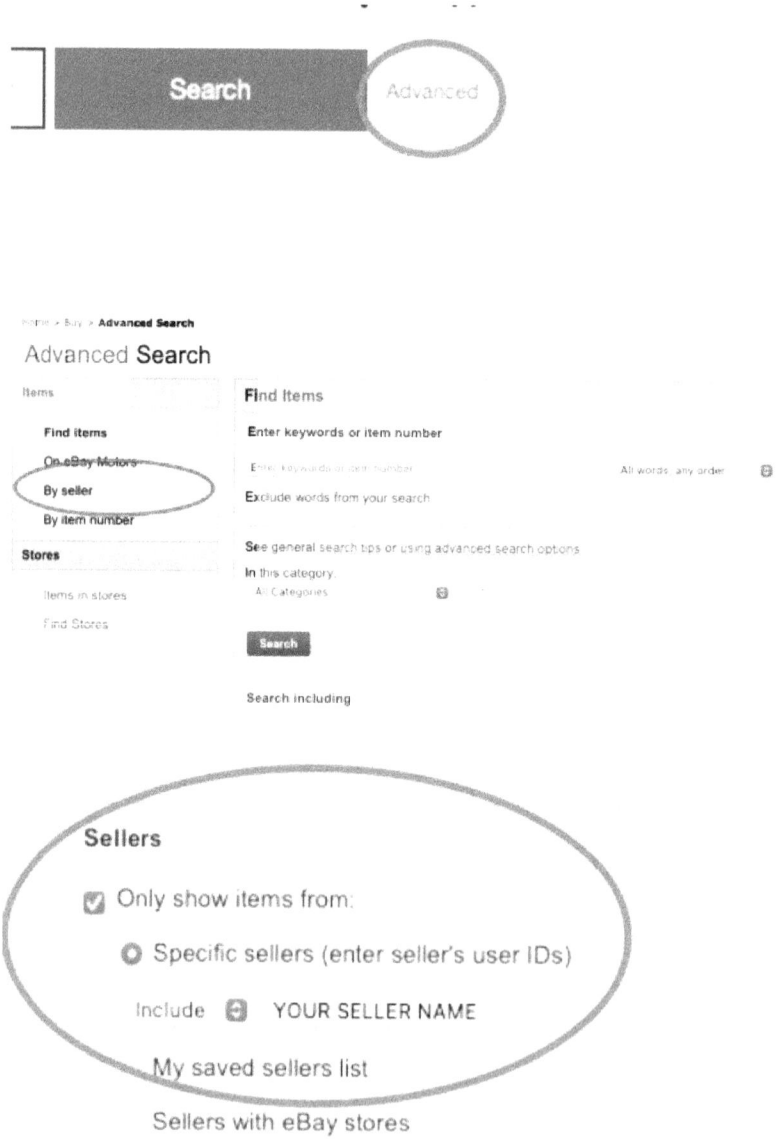

You can also use a service like LinkTree to create a single page for all of the links you want your customers to connect with on

Instagram. Learn more at https://linktr.ee

Hook People with your Bio

When people click on your Instagram account, they will see your bio info. Create a short bio with relevant information about yourself and your business. Don't oversell in the bio – make it light and interesting. Here's a good article on crafting a compelling bio. https://www.jennstrends.com/create-instagram-bio-draws-followers/

Warm Up Your Account

It will take some time to start seeing activity on your new Instagram account. Create your new account NOW and begin following other eBay users by searching for hashtags such as #eBay #ebayseller #shreseller, and more. As you see other hashtags being used, add these to your search. Follow, like, and comment on posts from these searches.

Use Popular Hashtags

When you post to Instagram, you'll want to include hashtags so your posts will come up in search results. Those hashtags should consist of the brand of the item you are sharing, along with #eBay, #ebayseller, and more. You can use services like Hashtagify.me to find popular hashtags.

Be Professional and Promote Your Brand

Your Instagram profile photo should be the same as your eBay Store photo, and all your posts should be related to your eBay business or your personal brand. From within the Instagram app, you can switch to a Business Profile. You will add credibility to your Instagram account and access analytics to help you make data-driven decisions. Go to Settings > Switch to business account.

Mix it Up

Once you've started getting followers, adding additional photos related to your eBay business, the brands you sell, your personal brand, or other related items are great ways to mix things up and make your Instagram feed more interesting. Many eBay IG users share their unique story of success on eBay to help connect with the community.

Be Consistent

Share or post to IG daily – multiple times if you can. Consistent interaction is the key to success. You will increase engagement with your followers and attract more new followers if you consistently post on Instagram. Using a service like Hootsuite to schedule posts is a great way to keep your feed active. With Hootsuite, you can schedule posts out for 30-days with their free plan and preview how everything will look.

You may be tempted to shortcut your Instagram growth by focusing just on the number of followers. Here's why that's not the best strategy:

When promoting and building your business on Instagram, it's easy to believe the follower myth. The follower myth promotes the belief that more is better, that growing the number of your followers is paramount to add credibility to your Instagram profile and to promote your brand.

Don't believe the Follower Myth

If your focus is primarily on building the number of followers, regardless of how relevant they are to your business, your results will be disappointing. This article will focus on the importance of finding relevant, high-quality followers who want to engage with your company and how to build your network with proven best practices.

Use your Existing Assets

Let's start with what you have. For existing businesses, think about your customer list, your existing newsletter, any methods you are using to connect with existing customers. If you have a retail presence, are you offering an incentive at checkout to keep the relationship going with your customers by getting their email or having them follow you on the spot? The key here is not to overlook the assets you already have – the customers that already love you are one of the best ways to seed your Instagram followers.

Research Keywords

The next step is to research what your potential customers are talking about on Instagram for both new and existing businesses. You can do this manually or by using services that specialize in digging through Instagram data.

#camping
22,785,934 posts

Manually, you can search for keywords on the Instagram website to see how many posts there are and how much activity is happening around a particular topic or brand. And just like followers, higher numbers aren't always better. A niche keyword active with a small but passionate group of Instagram users can often convert for you better than a broad keyword.

For example, if you are selling camping gear, let's say Tents for this example. Searching for the keyword #camping brings up over 22 million results. Dig deeper and search for #campting-tents to find a few thousand people using this keyword in their posts. Focusing on those few thousand will typically have a much higher success rate. Use this tactic to search for long-tail keywords that are relevant to your business or brand.

#campingtents
1,932 posts

Use a research service like Hashtagify or Leetags to automatically find niche keywords related to your brand or what you're trying to talk to your customers about. These services can help you find the right keywords to use in your Instagram posts to attract quality followers.

While we're on the topic of keywords, try not to clog up your posts with dozens of keywords. It's better to post more often with different keyword hashtags than it is to fill up a single post with tons of #hashtagthis and #hashtagthat. I also like to separate keywords from my content to keep things clean:

Post Quality Content and Add Value

You've done your research, you know what keywords you want

to target, and you're ready to go. That's awesome – one of the essential parts of success is just to START – don't wait for perfection; get going and iterate as you learn more and improve your Instagram posts.

While posting, keep in mind that social followers are typically not transactional. They want to have a relationship with your business or brand beyond just buying things from you. By posting quality content that is interesting, funny, beautiful, and perceived as adding value beyond just trying to make a sale, you will build a loyal following that will occasionally place an order.

Get Real and the 80/20 Rule

You can use the 80/20 rule and only focus on selling 20% of the time, while the other 80% is spent creating content that explores how your products are used. Include tips about your niche (think camping tips for the tent example above), posts about your employees and perhaps their interests, surveys, news, etc. Think about what you would like to see in your own

Instagram feed – what posts do you stop scrolling to learn some-thing, look deeper, like, and engage.

Be authentic

The BS detectors on social media are strong. Potential custom-ers want to have a relationship with companies, people, and brands that are real, not staged, and manipulative. Show your company lunch, post about an employee accomplishment, new addition to your staff, whatever – mix up your posts and be true to your company culture. This authenticity will cause like-minded people to gravitate towards your Instagram feed – these are much easier to convert to customers than someone who knows nothing about your business or brand.

Post Quality Images

You'll attract more quality followers by posting quality images on Instagram. Using a free service like Canva to design your posts is an easy way to make your feed stand out. Canva has thousands of templates to choose from, and you can integrate your photos, as well.

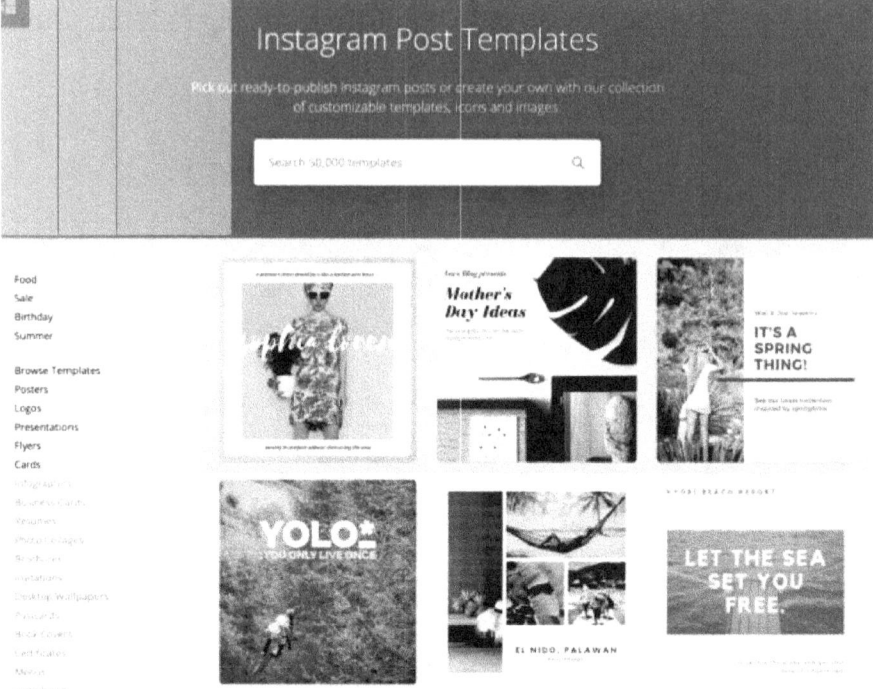

We love the idea of using your photos for your posts, but you might also consider using stock photos for certain types of posts or memes. Canva can help with that, or there are other free stock photo sites (search Google), and you may want to consider a paid stock photo site like Shutterstock.

Timing is important

Try posting on Instagram at different times and monitor how much engagement each post gets. Your followers may be more active in the early morning or later in the evening. Experiment and measure likes, comments, and follows to come up with your own best practices for the best time of the day to post.

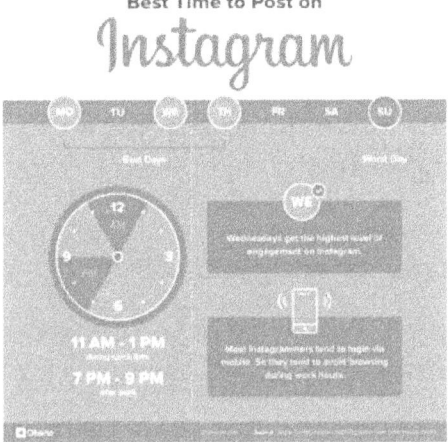

Use Instagram Stories

Instagram Stories are a powerful way to connect with your followers and significantly increase engagement on your account. Canva has some great tips on how to utilize their free service to create Instagram Stories that is worth a read.

Facebook

I am not a fan of using a Facebook personal page to promote your eBay business. Your friends and family will quickly get tired of seeing your posts. Instead, create a Facebook business page to promote your eBay listings and your business specifically. You might also consider creating a Facebook group that is related to the types of products you sell.

To create a Facebook business page, start here: https://www.facebook.com/business/pages/set-up

Use the same tactics that I described above with Pinterest and Instagram. The 80/20 rule should be in effect as well.

To create a Facebook group, start here: https://www.facebook.com/help/167970719931213/

Sharing your eBay listings on social media

When you have your Pinterest, Instagram, and Facebook channels setup, there are quick methods to share your product listings directly with each channel. Keep that 80/20 rule in mind
since you don't want to bombard people with just your listings.
Work your listings into the regular flow or quality posts that
you are making.

Share an eBay product listing manually

Go to one of your product listings. You will see the Twitter,
Facebook, and Pinterest logos in the upper right corner of the
page.

Be sure you are logged into your personal Facebook account,
then click the Facebook logo. A window will open for you to
enter some text about the item and select where to post. If you
don't make any location selection, the product listing will post
to your personal Facebook page. Once you setup your Facebook
business page or group, you can select to post there.

To share a product listing on Pinterest, click the Pinterest logo. Be sure you are logged into your Pinterest business account. A new window will open, and you can select which Board to Pin the link to.

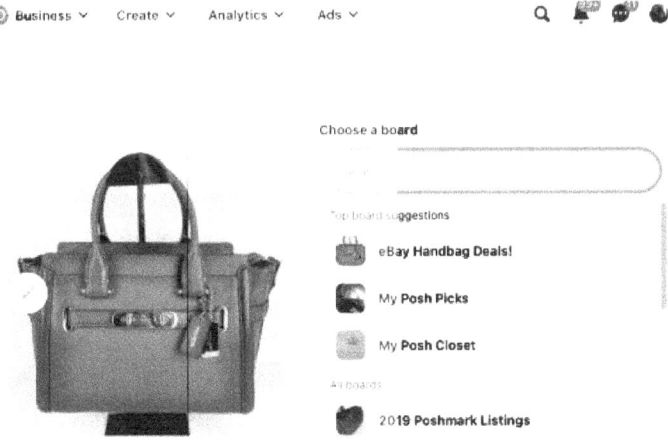

eBay does not have a direct Instagram share link. You will need to create your Instagram posts manually or with an automation app like HootSuite. There is an excellent article on additional eBay strategies for Instagram on the eBay community board:

https://community.ebay.com/t5/eBay-for-Business/The-Complete-Guide-to-Marketing-Your-eBay-Items-on-

Instagram/ba-p/28004086

Social is always changing, and I encourage you to experiment and measure the impact of different tactics to promote your eBay store. The main takeaways from this chapter are to get some exposure, build followers, and add value to your followers with quality posts.

IS THIS THE END OR JUST THE BEGINNING?

This may be the end of eBay Unlocked, but I hope it is just the beginning of your long-term success on eBay! I also hope you found the book useful and that eBay Unlocked becomes part of your toolkit for success.

You're Awesome

The fact that you read through this book and are taking the required actions to create a success system on eBay is a big deal. Starting is the hardest part. Most people just talk, but you have taken action to build your business and to find success!

Words are cheap. Action builds wealth.

It is this action that will create your success story on eBay. **Actionable steps, however small, taken every-single-day are what it takes to succeed.** It will be hard, there are no shortcuts, but I am confident in your ability to take what you have learned in eBay Unlocked to create the business you want. Whatever sales level you want to be at, however many orders you want to ship – you can do it, and I am here to help.

Connect with me

Let's keep in touch! You can and should connect with me in the Unlocked Resellers Group, on LinkedIn, and via email.

Join the private Unlocked Resellers Group to help grow your eBay business:
https://www.facebook.com/groups/poshmarkunlocked

Connect with me on LinkedIn
https://www.linkedin.com/in/shannonjjean/

Send me an email: me@shannonjean.com

Listen to me

As you can probably tell, I love talking about Small Business topics. I am fortunate to be able to co-host The Small Business Show podcast each week. We have over 300 episodes of content, interviews, tips, and what we like to call Business Therapy. There is a wealth of information and learning to be found in our archives from the past 6-years. I encourage you to subscribe to The Small Business Show at https://businessshow.co

Share your story

I want to hear from you. Share your story in the Unlocked Re-seller Group, send me an email, and tell me what I missed in eBay Unlocked, what I got wrong, and anything else you want to talk about. **The best part of my business life is the interaction that I get to have with like-minded entrepreneurs that lift each other up to be more successful.**

I am so looking forward to hearing about your success, and I can't wait to see you soon in the Unlocked Reseller Group!

Cheers!

Shannon Jean
Lafayette, CA
February 2021

www.ingramcontent.com/pod-product-compliance
Lightning Source LLC
Chambersburg PA
CBHW070328220526
45467CB00001B/74